THE ESTUARY'S GIFT

THE ESTUARY'S GIFT

AN ATLANTIC COAST CULTURAL BIOGRAPHY

THE PENNSYLVANIA STATE UNIVERSITY PRESS
UNIVERSITY PARK, PENNSYLVANIA

DAVID GRIFFITH

RURAL STUDIES SERIES
Michael D. Schulman, General Editor

The Estuary's Gift: An Atlantic Coast Cultural Biography, David Griffith

Library of Congress Cataloging-in-Publication Data

Griffith, David Craig, 1951–
The estuary's gift : an Atlantic Coast cultural biography / David Griffith.
p. cm.—(Rural studies series)
Includes bibliographical references and index.
ISBN 0-271-01950-6 (cloth : alk. paper)
ISBN 0-271-01951-4 (paper : alk. paper)
1. Maritime anthropology—Middle Atlantic States. 2. Maritime
anthropology—United States—Atlantic Coast. 3. Fishing villages—
Middle Atlantic States. 4. Fishing villages—United States—
Atlantic Coast. 5. Coastal ecology—Middle Atlantic States.
6. Coastal ecology—United States—Atlantic Coast. 7. Middle
Atlantic States—Social conditions. 8. Atlantic Coast (U.S.)—
Social conditions. I. Title. II. Series: Rural studies series
(University Park, Pa.)
GN560.M63G75 1999
306'.0974—dc21
99-29265
CIP

It is the policy of The Pennsylvania State University Press
to use acid-free paper for the first printing of all clothbound books.
Publications on uncoated stock satisfy the minimum requirements
of American National Standard for Information Sciences—
Permanence of Paper for Printed Library Materials, ANSI Z39.48–1992.

FOR TWO WISE MEN

Bill Queen
and
B. J. Copeland

CONTENTS

LIST OF ILLUSTRATIONS

PREFACE

A net ban in Florida and a ground-fishing crisis in New England moved several state legislators in Mid-Atlantic Coast states to protect their own fisheries. In 1994, for example, North Carolina legislators placed a moratorium on issuing new fishing licenses while they learned more about the state's fisheries. They commissioned several studies of the state's fishing industry, all of which were scheduled to be completed during an election year: 1996. This timing was unfortunate. Elected officials can have difficulty thinking clearly while their jobs are at stake. They waffle, they make promises, they contradict themselves and apologize for previous positions, quite often they lie. If these behaviors send mixed signals to voters, imagine how confused those they appoint to chair special committees, let alone the people whom their legislating will most likely affect, must be. Is it any wonder such committee heads often sift through research findings for bits and evidence to support their constituents' positions, ignoring facts and positions that aren't in line with the recommendations of the powerful?

One casualty of such proceedings is science. Whether scientists report their findings in ways designed to support predetermined political decisions, or politicians discount facts staring them straight in the face, science placed in the service of politics inevitably suffers. This book emerges from my concerns about the ways politicians, journalists, scientists themselves, and others who have some kind of stake in the direction of the development of the Mid-Atlantic coastal plain, have used science. It is also a personal response to the social science literature produced on Mid-Atlantic fisheries. Too often, these are merely technical reports that do not represent fishing families, the fishing industry, or coastal history, although there are notable exceptions. Especially flawed are the studies on the economics of fisheries or policy issues that draw conclusions based on faulty assumptions, misinterpreted data, and bias.

This book is not as much a work of science as a cultural biography. It is a descriptive yet theoretically informed work about the past and the future of coastal development, highlighting the lives of some of the individuals who have contributed to that past and will contribute to that future. Through the lens of the history and contemporary problems of the Mid-Atlantic Coast (primarily focusing on North Carolina yet also including information on Maryland's lower eastern shore, Virginia, and the Chesapeake), this book develops the idea that environmental degradation follows the loss of the intimate understandings of coastal ecosystems that fishing families possess. Assaults on commercial fishing families—whether from organized recreational interests, real estate developers, or public policy makers—reduce the social and cultural diversity of the coast, upsetting the balance of rights and obligations we achieve with the giving and receiving of gifts. What I chronicle along the coast are developments that erode families and communities across American landscapes: the wearing away of local and regional history that results when national retail and restaurant chains convert local merchants into clerks and busboys, or the loss of biological diversity that follows the reconfiguration of countrysides to support monocrop agriculture, industrial chicken production, hog farming, forestry, and mining.

The book's eight interlocking essays draw out the lessons of biological diversity and environmental balance that come from the ways the Algonquins named bodies of water and from families who have trapped crabs and drifted gill nets for herring since the first European migrations south out of Jamestown. The essays are, as well, ever cognizant of the complexities of ecological relationships and the natural peace and beauty of the wetlands, estuaries, bottoms, and even the cluttered spaces of working docks and fish houses.

The book attempts to insert human relations into natural cycles by considering the ways we treat one another in light of the ways we treat nature, measuring both by the standards we invoke when we give and receive gifts. Stories of conflicts among fishers, of Mexican immigrant women brought into seafood houses to pick the meat from cooked, cooled crab—displacing and replacing poor African-American women—and of the slow yet steady attempts to criminalize family fishing practices that reach back thirteen generations show the ways that the rights, obligations, and responsibilities of gift exchange have eroded. While I do not claim to develop a systematic analysis of exchange theory in this volume, I do hope that my use of gift exchange as an overarching metaphor for the human relations of coastal heritage will encourage others to reconsider how we think about coastal development. By extension, I hope that the theme of gift exchange, elaborated through the history and experiences of working families, will encourage more people to question many of the structural developments and seemingly inevitable economic processes that threaten to commoditize nearly everything we hold dear. It has become far too easy to dismiss alternatives to established trajectories of business, finance, and government as overly romantic, without considering that such dismissals reinforce those trajectories while diminishing our capacity to develop alternatives to them. More than an account of the decline of fishing families or a stressed natural resource, these essays illustrate how pressing social problems such as environmental degradation and assaults on working families play out in local contexts and in local history.

The concerns from which these essays emerge are shared, I believe, by many of the fishing families along the Atlantic Coast, as well as many of those of us who love the waters of Eastern North Carolina and who lament the horrors of deteriorating water quality that currently plague our rivers and sounds. We live with several environmental threats: forestry, pulp and paper milling, phosphate mining interests, municipal sewage discharge, industrial farming operations, and the looming possibility of ever larger animal processing facilities along the rivers that feed the estuaries. Ironically, much of the diverting of public attention away from pressing environmental problems is done in the name of environmentalism, as groups of activists focus disproportionately on one or two issues at the expense of a more holistic view of the estuary and every-one's role in its health. Many politicians support environmental degrada-tion in the name of progress, weighing the creation of jobs against the destruction of forests or the pollution of our waters and lands, or sup-porting one environmental issue because it diverts attention from others. Usually their arguments ignore the ways in which this so-called progress achieves exactly what it is supposed to counteract, reducing the eco-nomic diversity that allows regions, communities, neighborhoods, and families to develop their own economic opportunities rather than be-come dependent upon large, multistate and multinational social struc-tures that have no allegiance to any local area.

These processes, left unchecked, will surely result in our resembling, more and more, a Third World nation of cheap labor with a ruined environment. Commercial fishing families of the Mid-Atlantic represent a stronghold against these processes, a symbol of social and economic diversity and ties to local history and local ecosystems that build upon self-sufficiency and independence. They represent an alternative to the empty promises of firms that invade communities, press for tax holidays, feed off the support of municipal sewer, water, police, and school sys-tems, reorganize environments, and then leave at a moment's notice with little more to show for their presence than contaminated lots and families of laid-off and injured workers with mortgages and medical bills.

Some of the individuals who provided words and information for this book are still deeply engaged in opposing those who continue to assault and support the assaults on the estuary. To protect their identities, I give the fishers quoted and described throughout this volume pseud-onyms, as is common in my profession and highly recommended by my university's Human Subjects Review Committee. Each name used, however, refers to a specific individual; I don't doubt that a few of them will be able to recognize themselves and their words. I tampered with their words only slightly, when they were repeating themselves or strayed too far from a point, but in most cases the quotations come directly from taped interviews without significant editing.

I have not, by contrast, altered the names of other anthropologists and various colleagues whose work I mention, and the few public figures mentioned in the volume are well enough known that I tend not to refer to them by name at all, but by their position or their behavior.

Perhaps because the essays in this book are somewhat personal and are calculated to engage the reader, I chose to suspend the academic conventions of both parenthetical citations and footnotes throughout the text. Instead, I discuss the sources used for this work in a separate bibliographic essay at the end.

ACKNOWLEDGMENTS

As usual, I have become indebted to several individuals during the course of writing this volume, primarily the fishers and others who spent so much of their time talking with me or with one of my research assistants. Susan West, one of the most articulate fishing industry activists in the state, a fisher herself from Buxton, North Carolina, was kind enough to review an earlier draft of this book and offer excellent constructive criticism. Charles and Mildred Gilgo, fishers from Atlantic, North Carolina, provided interesting interpretations of policy decisions dealing with coastal issues and offered their own oral histories of Down East North Carolina on more than one occasion.

Much of the information regarding the biology and sociology of the coast came from my fellow scientists at East Carolina University's Institute for Coastal and Marine Resources, who have tolerated my at times foolish curiosity with the skillful and patient teaching that comes from conducting research with the painstaking effort that science requires: Lisa Clough, Margie Gallagher, Jeff Johnson, Joseph Luszcovich, Roger Rulifson, and Don Stanley. Also helpful were the highly skilled Cindy Harper and Kay Evans, who provided me with several forms of professional and emotional support as the Institute's cornerstone personnel. And, of course, I am indebted to Bill Queen, the Institute's director, to whom this work is dedicated, for his unflagging support of my work, his inspiring leadership skill, and his wisdom in things academic, scientific, and practical. I know no one more qualified to design or plan, whether it be a new Ph.D. program, a research proposal, or the expansion of a driveway.

In the anthropology department I learned a great deal about coastal

ACKNOWLEDGMENTS

Native American populations from John Byrd, Randy Daniel, Charles Ewen, Dale Hutchinson, and David Phelps. I have also benefited from being colleagues with Loraine Aragon, John Bort, Bob Bunger, Barbara Garrity-Blake, Holly Mathews, and Linda Wolfe. Over the past few years I have been lucky enough to serve on the Southern Coastal Heritage Committee, where I have learned a great deal about coastal heritage from Candy Beal, Jim Clark, Jeffrey Crow, Sondra Kirsch, Carmine Prioli, Keats Sparrow, and Lundy Spence. Patrick Stanforth, John Brown, and Douglas Hobbs provided research assistance for many of the projects that provided information for this book. Vernon Kelley, a fine sociologist, has been an enduring friend and incredibly skillful research associate on nearly all of my research projects. I have always relied heavily on his keen ability to establish a rapport among individuals from a wide variety of occupational, class, and ethnic backgrounds, and I simply could not have completed much of the research I have without him.

At the North Carolina Department of Cultural Resources, I thank Earl Iames, who helped me select most of the photographs in the volume, as well as Kathy Hart, formerly with the University of North Carolina Sea Grant College Program. Most of the research for this book was funded by the Sea Grant College Program. Indeed, with the exception of the opening and closing chapters, each of the other chapters is based on material collected during one of six projects over the course of the past ten years. On most of these projects I worked with my good friend Jeff Johnson, and others as co-investigators or associates: Walter Clark, Margie Gallagher, Barbara Garrity-Blake, and James Murray. I hold none of them responsible for any mistakes that may appear here, however. Nor could I possibly hold responsible the anonymous reviewers for Penn State Press, who offered several excellent suggestions for the revision of the manuscript. Funds from the National Science Foundation contributed to Chapter 4 (SBR-9706637) and Chapter 7 (DBS-9211620). Other sponsors of this work have been the Ford Foundation, the National Marine Fisheries Service, the Howard Heinz Foundation, the National Park Service, and the U.S. Department of Labor. North Carolina Legal

Services provided me with transcripts and other materials concerning the trial discussed in Chapter 4. I am also indebted for ideas in this chapter to Luis Torres and Monica Heppel, with whom I have conducted several studies of workers with H-2 visas, and to the organizations that funded my doctoral dissertation work in Jamaica and the apple- and sugar-growing regions of the United States: Fulbright-Hays, the Inter-American Foundation, and the Wenner-Grenn Foundation for Anthropological Research. My deepest thanks go to all these organizations for their continued trust in my work.

Finally, a few personal acknowledgments: My friend Monica Heppel rented me her beach house in Nags Head for next to nothing, for a week, where I was able to thoroughly edit the manuscript. I thank her and her beach house. And I could not have completed much of this, or anything else, without the love and support of my wife, Nancy, whose literary taste surpasses that of almost everyone I know, including many of the faculty members of English departments I have encountered over the years. She gave an early draft of the manuscript a thorough reading and even asked to read it again, and I took her comments to heart and to the page. My daughters, Emily and Brook, now young adults, have tolerated my absences for research and provided me with countless hours of humor and pleasant companionship. I love them dearly and hope they will find something here in return for their gifts of amusement.

ESTUARIES
AND
GIFTS

Where is the sea, that once solved the whole loneliness
Of the Midwest?
—James Wright

The first time Daniel slows to rest, breathing hard, the soft, damp earth gives beneath his bare feet and he knows he has crossed into the land the Meherrin people call pocosin. It feels the way a miracle might feel, telling him he is close to the Great Dismal Swamp, where other fugitive slaves wait for chances to move to Edenton or Norfolk and board ships bound for the open sea or the Chesapeake. He is used to traveling at night, from the many nights he crossed through woodlands to attend worship services with other slaves on neighboring plantations. Now, after running, he moves more slowly, listening for changes in the songs of owls that signal the presence of others, zigzagging over the wet landscape in a way that, he prays, will confuse the bloodhounds.

It's doubtful they miss him yet, but they will soon, very soon. It's been six hours since he left the timber camp near the Roanoke, but a full year since he came up with the idea of escaping during the height of the herring run, when everyone from the plantation crowded the riverbank to work the mule-driven seines and cut and salt the fish. It's 1857. The legs of his trousers still hold the scent of the fish, lingering among odors of pine sap, rosin, tar, and pitch from his turns at the turpentine distillery, when the Harringtons rented him out to smaller planters between Roanoke and Chowan.

It was while working on a smaller plantation that he learned from other slaves about secret networks linking families north and south along the coast, people who would harbor fugitives slaves and ferry them across the wilds of Albemarle, Pamlico, and Chesapeake, into the mouth of the Pocomoke River to Snow Hill, Maryland, hugging the Delaware coast into Philadelphia.

But Daniel knows that years could pass before a free black waterman helps him secure passage on a vessel. More immediate matters gnaw at him. As dawn approaches, as his shift is to begin at the haul seines that work from sunrise to sunrise through the season, all day, all night, the time they will discover him missing draws near. With the morning light he hopes to find the community of fugitive slaves hidden deep in the swamp. He has known about that community since he was a child, without knowing any more about them than that they live on islands inside the swamp and that, twice in his memory, bounty hunters went in with their dogs and guns and returned empty and whipped, unwilling to marshal a second attack.

He moves slowly through the cypress. As daylight grows he hears, in the distance, a faint human disturbance of the forest. Moving in that direction, he smells the wood smoke of burning juniper and begins to hear chopping sounds. He moves closer, until he can see that all but three of the crew are black men, felling cypress tress and cutting shingles. Half of the day he watches them, waiting. Shortly after noon one of them moves away from the group and Daniel sneaks to a place between him and the others. When the man returns to the timber crew, Daniel intercepts him, gently, so as not to startle him, and says, "Can you help me?"

Slowly a smile comes to the other man's face.

At night along Albemarle, overnight camps of black watermen spring up between the plantations and towns. "They'll know," says Conrad, the cypress worker

Daniel has befriended. Daniel was just the excuse Conrad had been waiting for. It was as though he hadn't realized he was waiting for anything until Daniel rose, as if from the earth, between him and the others. And then his name was Daniel. Of the lion's den. That's when Conrad chose to leave with him during the night.

They seek out the spontaneous camps of watermen who tie flat-bottomed craft to the bank and gather around a fire, cooking eels, boiling wild mustard greens, exchanging stories about the most recent shoals in the waterway.

It's not as simple as it might seem. Among them there may be one who needs the favor or bounty of turning in fugitive slaves. But the risk is less here, along this isolated stretch of Albemarle, than it would be in Edenton or Elizabeth City, where authorities lurk along the waterfront, checking papers of passage, watching for any black man who doesn't belong.

Here along Albemarle, their best friend is the terrain—places where the wind-driven waters meet cypress and carve out a sheltered bay, build a narrow strip of beach, and mist the soggy earth entangled in the shadows of soft woods and shallow pools of rainwater. It is this terrain that allows them to creep to the edge of the encampment of watermen and listen to their voices, gleaning from the tones and words signs of strength and compassion, or weakness and treachery, that will tell them which of the watermen to approach.

By full nightfall they have chosen a man who speaks with a soft measured voice, gazes across the water thoughtfully, and sips his whiskey more judiciously than the others. Before first light they wake him without disturbing the others. He knows what they want immediately. The first words he utters to them are: "You can trust me."

Those words resonate in their minds inside the hull of the steamer, heading north, safe, hidden among the barrels of salted herring, corn dried over wood smoke, tobacco and winter wheat.

During the turbulent last decades of slavery, an enslaved freight captain named Peter was one of a handful of local sailors who knew the waters of the Cape Fear River intimately enough to pilot vessels in and out of Wilmington Harbor, guiding cargoes of rice, turpentine, cotton, and tobacco to the edge of the sea lanes. He mistrusted official nautical surveys of the coastline because of the fickle nature of the river. With great skill he avoided the river's shoals and found ever-shifting channels out of the harbor, becoming so indispensable to commerce that he commandeered his independence to ferry escaped slaves out of the South and onto ships bound for New England—an overwater link in the underground railroad.

Peter was not alone among watermen, black and white, who helped slaves to freedom over an intricate network of swamps, estuaries, rivers, harbors, bays, and sounds that extended from Cape Fear south to the Savannah River and north into the Chesapeake Bay. Between the southern tip of North Carolina's coast and the mouth of the Chesapeake, intricate waterways in and out of the Pamlico and Albemarle Sounds aided these clandestine operations. From inland plantations, fugitive slaves followed the Cape Fear, Neuse, Tar, Pamlico, Roanoke, and Chowan Rivers to coastal settlements where, with luck and sometimes after months or years of hiding, they acquired passage to freedom. Like Daniel and Conrad, their freedom depended on sound judgment and close observation, along with creativity and perseverance. One of the most famous and patient was Harriet Jacobs, who hid for years in an Edenton attic, awaiting passage. On the Delmarva Peninsula, east of the Chesapeake, Harriet Tubman helped slaves to freedom with the assistance of people as far apart as free black riverboat captains of Maryland's Pocomoke River and Union officers stationed on the sea islands of South Carolina.

These are only two of the more famous cases. An abolitionist in Philadelphia, William Still, collected hundreds of escaped slaves' accounts of ingenious and difficult passages along the underground railroad. Experiences on ships leaving North Carolina were particularly harrowing. To prevent slave stowaways, North Carolina legislators passed a law requiring that all vessels be thoroughly inundated with smoke before leaving port. After probing the sympathies of a ship captain bound for Philadelphia, Abram Galloway and Richard Eden, two slaves from Wilmington, improvised gas masks and stowed away on a vessel carrying tar, rosin, and turpentine. "This safe-guard," Still writes about the gas masks, "consisted of silk oil cloth shrouds, made large, with drawing strings, which, when pulled over their heads, might be drawn very tightly around their waists, whilst the process of smoking was in operation." Despite these precautions, the vessel was never smoked, but the effects of the turpentine cargo proved worse than any smoke, causing them to bleed from "every pore in frightful quantities." They arrived in Philadelphia near death, but gradually recovered with the help of Still and his Vigilance Committee.

Coastal environments lend themselves to clandestine enterprises and resistance. Navigable waterways from the Caribbean to the Gulf of Maine wind around islands, peninsulas, marshes, and other landscapes of protection, providing hiding places for slaves, pirates, smugglers, poachers, and, today, illegal immigrants and refugees. Some of the earliest inhabitants of coastal North Carolina and Virginia—the Secotan, Croatan, Pocomoke, and Nanticoke peoples—managed to elude the imperial expansion of Powhatan's confederacy because of their familiarity with swamps and waterways. And because collusion encourages and inspires equality, historically, at sea, the prejudices of race and ethnicity faded into the background as navigation skills and the crew's coordinated tasks faced open ocean. It was not entirely fictional for Melville's Ishmael to befriend, so completely, Queequeg—"on the whole a clean, comely looking cannibal."

In the U.S. South and the West Indies before emancipation, slaves who fished for the plantations enjoyed an independence unknown to field hands and house servants, using their sailing skills to engage in contraband trade while keeping their masters' kitchens stocked with fresh grouper, mackerel, and octopus. Puerto Rican watermen today use fishing as a therapy for the injuries they receive from temporary work in construction, meat packing, and other hazardous jobs on the mainland. In prehistoric times, oceans, wetlands, and coastal landscapes gave Native Americans gifts of stable food supplies and opportunities to settle that they never knew on the High Plains or in the deep boreal forests of the Appalachian Chain. The seacoast played a key role in the development of agriculture in the Mid-Atlantic Coast region, where an abundance of year-round fish and shellfish allowed people to settle long enough to learn the reproductive habits of local animals and plants. When John White encountered the Algonquin people, he found people who mixed farming and fishing so successfully that they were rarely without food.

Seacoasts still test the limits and potential of human qualities we value highly: independence, hard work, and the skill and vigilance it takes to read nature's signs and respond to her calls and warnings with agility and balance. Fishers today continue to hunt their prey, express independence, and resist the confines of political and economic institutions they consider as illegitimate and ludicrous as Daniel and Peter considered slavery. People raised on shifting landscapes and fluctuating populations of fish and shellfish acquire a cynicism toward new laws infringing on their life on the water, laws designed to freeze fishing practices in time and space or to restrict the use of gears that families have used for centuries, cutting away their individual rights as though they were lengths of whale bone once used as hoops inside women's skirts. At times fishers ignore new laws in such numbers that regulatory and enforcement agencies become forced to reconsider the laws themselves.

Fishers understand, of course, the need to protect fish, marine mammals, turtles, waterfowl, and coastal environments themselves. Protecting these resources is vital to their way of life. Most fishers rooted in their local coastal environments have ways of conserving resources, protecting nursery areas, and monitoring and regulating passage along waterways, but they have come to mistrust the motives of lawmakers, commissions, lobbyists, zoning boards, special councils, and the dozens of organizations that have emerged to assume control of the fate of the nation's coasts. Too often fisheries scientists make false assumptions or use theories that don't apply to fishing families. Too often those who would drain estuaries, destroy primary nursery areas, or order the disposal of toxins in waterways receive legal assistance from judges, commissioners, and state legislators who stand to benefit politically or financially, sacrificing the well-being of the many for the gain of a few.

By contrast, seacoasts and fishing lifestyles encourage the responsibilities of community. Fishers and farmers come together to trade the fruits of their work. Families join to weave, set, haul, and mend nets. Ever since the earliest European fisheries in North Carolina—the late winter and spring herring runs on the Chowan—men have captured and women have processed the herring. In like fashion, today, the winter scallop fisheries bring together families of fishers and their neighbors at Salter Path and Harkers Island. The general rule has always been that men dredge and bulk package the scallops, and women open them and extract the meats, but preparing the catch for market brings whole families into shucking houses along the coast. When the catch is successful and the price of the delicate white meats high, these divisions of labor break down: wives fish with husbands, and men join daughters, wives, and mothers at wooden cubicles inside the shucking houses.

Both entire families and whole communities gather around the harvesting and processing of many Mid-Atlantic fish and shellfish. In shucking houses, crab-picking plants, and herring salting and packing facilities, members of fishing households come together with others who are attached to the coast by different threads. Take Sally Kennelson's crab-picking plant near Lake Mattamuskeet in North Carolina's Hyde County. Sally has bright eyes, straight blond hair, a warm presence. In her office above the plant, the odors from the coffee pot and kitchenette always contain a hint of the smell of cooked crab. This aroma is both distinctive and difficult to describe. At its worst, near the dehydration plants of Pamlico County, it sears the nostrils and eyes as powerfully as any rotting flesh, but at its mildest it resembles the steam of a clambake enhanced with an odor like scalded milk. Sally's office smells like most crab-plant offices, closer to the mild boiled milk odor than the searing pungency. From this fishy chamber Sally calls merchants and keeps in touch with crabbers and truckers. Like most processing plants in the state, Sally's is a family operation, founded by her and her two brothers—both crabbers—in the mid-1980s.

Sally was an accountant, recently divorced, and running her own small consulting business when she saw the need for a crab-processing operation to serve crabbers along a 30-mile stretch of shoreline where the Pamlico Sound's waters meet the Pungo and Pamlico Rivers. She and her brothers built the concrete block facility and took turns, the first season, running the business, crabbing, accounting, and trying to live their lives. Opening and running a crab-processing facility is not something just anyone can do in their spare time. Add to this that Sally was a single woman entering a business long dominated by either men or families, and it is just short of miraculous that Sally made it through a single season.

Sally's success involved drawing on family and community reserves that would have tried anyone's patience. That Sally's brothers were crabbers helped when it came to getting crabbers to supply crabs to the plant, but other problems arose from the nature of picking meat from steamed blue crabs. I interviewed dozens of processing-plant owners and crab pickers in the mid-1980s, around the time Sally and her brothers were opening their plant. At that time nearly everyone in the industry agreed that the skill and patience it took to pick crabmeat were dying crafts. Young women were simply not replacing their mothers, aunts, and grandmothers in plants like Sally's, breaking with—or freeing themselves from—a tradition that was several decades old. Statistics on crab processing during that period show that the labor force was shrinking. Some crab plants closed because they could not recruit pickers. In autumn of 1993, in a crab plant in Oriental, Alexander J., an African-American gentleman, complained to me of having to go out into the neighborhoods to get pickers to come to work during this low point in the labor supply. "I used to have to beg for pickers if we had a big load of crab," he said. "Beg for 'em!"

Faced with the problem of finding local pickers, Sally joined other crab processors in Virginia, Maryland, and North Carolina and turned to Mexico for crab pickers. In 1988, Sally began bringing in women from Tabasco, a coastal state just west of the Yucatan Peninsula. Today these women sit before piles of cooked and cooled blue crabs and fill Sally's plastic quart-size tubs with the succulent white meat. Now, instead of the old spirituals, at the picking tables you hear songs of "*amor*" and "*triste.*"

In less than ten years, Sally created an international community inside remote wetlands and cornfields of Hyde County. It is a mix of old and new, of the family ties and provincialism of the crabbing community enhanced with Mexican, Anglo, and African-American women and men coming together to produce one of the water's sweetest meats. There are still kinks in the society Sally has assembled—the homesickness of the Mexican women, the inevitable complaints of the narrow-minded about the influx of foreigners—but the threads with which Sally has stitched families of North Carolina crabbers together with families of Tabasco women are enriching and expanding human communication.

So much of what we witness in seacoast communities is embedded in hidden nests of human and natural relationships, like those we see in Sally's crab-picking plant. Watching a crabber lift his pots and shake blue crabs into a plastic barrel, who would think that this decades-old process depended on young women coming from seacoast villages more than 2,000 miles away? Yet these complex and distant linkages exist, drawing families of commercial fishers into networks that include merchants along the Baltimore and New York waterfronts, marine biologists who monitor the health of the estuaries, paper-mill and mining executives who use rivers as private sewers, loons choking on oil balls, needlerushes tickling the storm clouds, and gulls whose egg shells tell of toxins in waters and winds. These linkages are based on exchanges of all kinds—familial, ecological, financial. These range from common and everyday exchanges, such as trading blue crabs or salted herring for engine repairs, to more complex exchanges seated in history and tradition. When a son acquires his father's familiarity with substrates, his sailing skill, and his knowledge of the habits and locations of fish, it is often in exchange for the son's promise to continue his father's way of life. In some ways these exchanges resemble those that take place in nature, as juvenile fish succumb to feeding seabirds so that others might benefit from the nutrients the seabirds defecate back into the estuary. Other exchanges are less beneficial, such as the trade-offs we sometimes make, foolishly, between water quality and the quarterly profits of corporations. Thus some exchanges are one-sided: some actors in the chain of relationships take and take without giving anything back. Usually, such behavior endangers the entire balance of relationships, endangering everyone. The French anthropologist Marcel Mauss, writing a slender volume called *The Gift,* a book about exchange in ancient societies, once said:

> To give something is to give a part of oneself. . . . One gives away what in reality is part of one's nature and substance, while to receive something is to receive a part of someone's spiritual essence. To keep this thing is dangerous, not only because it is illicit to do so, but because it comes morally, physically, and spiritually from a person. Whatever it is, food, possessions, women, children or ritual, it retains a magical and religious hold over the recipient.

All human societies have traditions of gift exchange similar to those Mauss describes. Mauss himself found examples of gift-giving from ethnohistorical accounts of peoples as distant from one another as the Tlingit and Haida of the Pacific Northwest, the Koryak of Siberia, and the Samoans, Maori, Tahitians, and Trobriand Islanders of the Pacific, linking gift-giving traditions among these hunter-gatherer and horticultural societies and those of Rome, Athens, India, Scandinavia, and his native France. He wrote with particular detail about the practice of Maori priests, who offered birds to the forest to enhance the gifts the forest would return, establishing a link between the forest and the very process of reproducing the Maori people and culture.

Similarly, canoe fishermen in Camurim, Brazil, offer packages of flowers, bits of cloth, and turtle-shell combs to the sea to break spells of poor fishing. Before the arrival of Europeans, during seasonal fairs and decennial celebrations called the Feast of the Dead, the Huron around the Great Lakes used ceremonial gift exchanges to cement ties between trading partners who provided necessities and luxury goods to villages scattered across a wide territory, drawing on the products of peoples inhabiting several ecological zones. Hunter-gatherers to the north provided furs, fish, and skins, and horticulturists to the south provided maize, tobacco, and hemp. The exchanges, to be sure, improved Huron standards of living, yet the trading that went on at these fairs was not simply the business of provisioning. Rituals accompanying the gift-giving at the Feasts of the Dead honored those who had died in the past ten years and publicly acknowledged new chiefs in a manner similar to swearing-in judges, ensuring the continuity of lineages across generations. Gift exchanges between new chiefs reinforced political alliances among the tribes.

Gift exchange remains a powerful force today. Most of us feel an obligation to give something back to someone who has given us a gift. As social creatures, we learn and teach the principles of generosity, responsibility, courtesy, and obligation. These vary from culture to culture, across time and space, but the spirit of the gift is found everywhere friendships are formed and relationships endure.

The feeling of obligation to return a gift of more or less equal meaning and value is part of the magical, spiritual essence that inhabits the gift. Gifts are part of the giver's self, his or her essence, because people choose gifts based on their relationship with the person to whom they give. Marjorie Kinnans Rawlings, describing her life in Cross Creek, a wet Florida environment of the 1930s, once wrote:

> I suppose there is nowhere in the world a more elemental exchange of goods than among ourselves at the Creek. The exchange does not even become barter and trade. We merely return favors. Old Boss uses my truck to haul his vegetable crops to the station and I use his mules for my occasional light plowing. We have never sat down to figure which has the higher rental value, for it does not matter. . . . One fisherman borrows a few dollars of me in lean times, and I have a drawing account for fish, never calculated exactly, but well tipped in my favor. Another man borrows between jobs and appears unsummoned when a freeze comes in and I must fire my young orange groves.

A little of the giver's thought and creativity goes into matching the appropriate gift with the recipient's needs and desires. This is why most of us are appalled when giving ceases to stimulate receiving, when the relationship becomes one-sided, withering in meaning and intensity. It then deteriorates and becomes business-like, a shadow of the former relationship, or it dies altogether. Yet if it persists, if it continues as an uneven relationship where one takes and takes without giving, it becomes, as Mauss said, dangerous. Linkages of obligation and responsibility break or fall out of balance, becoming polluting and destructive.

These breakdowns can occur in the relationships between humans and their environments as easily as between trading partners. When we receive an estuary's gifts without returning gifts of stewardship, resource conservation, and preservation—gifts that ultimately depend on the intimate understandings that derive from thinking of the estuary as a crucial part of our history and heritage—we endanger the estuary and thereby endanger our children and ourselves.

The expansive yet fragile nature of the Mid-Atlantic coastline deepens the risk of these breakdowns happening. The basic statistics are impressive. The Chesapeake Bay constitutes the largest estuary on the eastern seaboard, well chronicled in such books as *Chesapeake*, by James Michener, and William Warner's *Beautiful Swimmers*. By comparison, North Carolina's coast is less well known. Its heart is the Albemarle-Pamlico Estuarine System, an area of 2,900 square miles that is second in size only to the Chesapeake along the eastern seaboard. The system consists of two drowned river valleys, along with their tributaries and surrounding wetlands, forests, and sandier, inhabitable islands, including North Carolina's well-known Outer Banks. East of the Suffolk Scarp, a ridge of old barrier island shoreline defining the geological boundary between the piedmont and coastal plain, the coast's entire being is marine. Its very foundation comes from the sea. Marine sediments of shells and fish bones, gravel, sands, peat, and minerals are up to 3 kilometers thick at Cape Hatteras and 600 meters deep closer to the Scarp. Millennia ago, during one of the interglacial periods where the earth was warmer and the polar ice caps were far, far smaller, the waters of Albemarle and Pamlico mingled with those of the Chesapeake to the north and the Cape Fear River to the south.

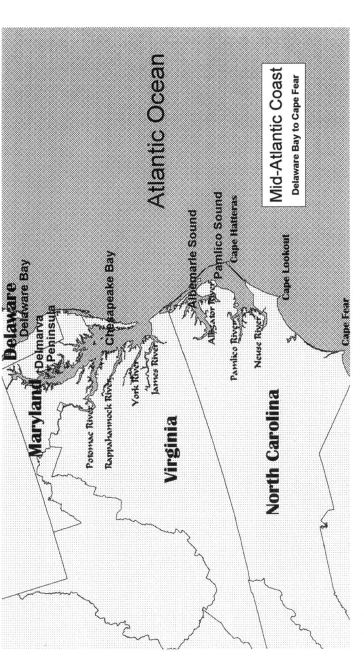

Mid-Atlantic Coast, Delaware Bay to Cape Fear

Even today, several common threads—natural and human in origin—join the waters of North Carolina with those of the Chesapeake. Both support large populations of blue crabs, watermen, and the crab-processing houses that import Mexican women. Both drink from overlapping watersheds. Both suffer from the runoffs of agriculture, the dioxins of paper manufacture, the sulfuric acid produced by phosphate mining, the eroding landscapes of forestry, the choking blooms of algae. Whether you visit the Alligator River Preserve in North Carolina or the Black Water Preserve on Maryland's lower eastern shore, you will see the same tundra swans, geese, pintails, buffleheads, and canvasbacks that, in both regions, spawned decoy-carving traditions that have transcended the mere desire to lure and kill waterfowl, inspiring works of art.

Cape Hatteras forms a natural boundary between northern and southern waters, preventing many South Atlantic species from moving farther north and many North Atlantic species from moving farther south. If you think of North Carolina's shape as a hatchet, with the blunt end facing west and the sharp edge facing east, the hatchet's first point to penetrate its mark would be Cape Hatteras. Anglers heading north out of Hatteras encounter schools of pollock and hake, while those turning south run into the grouper, snapper, and billfish of the Gulf Stream. The watersheds of the rivers of eastern North Carolina encompass major portions of central North Carolina and southeastern Virginia. Together, Albemarle and Pamlico Sounds draw on more than 30,000 square miles of watershed, fed by such impressive streams as the Roanoke, the Chowan, the Pungo, the Alligator, and the Neuse Rivers. Nearly 50,000 cubic feet of water spill into these sounds every second. In Albemarle Sound the water changes completely every six weeks, and in the Pamlico Sound every fourteen weeks.

Yet for all its expanse and diversity, the Albemarle-Pamlico Estuarine system is, throughout, relatively shallow, its deepest point less than 30 feet and its average depth between 11 and 16 feet. Sandbars and shoals hinder easy navigation, forming and reforming over time, shifting with currents, winds, and rains. Roanoke Inlet, once entered by John White and at one time the most important inlet on the coast, was choking with

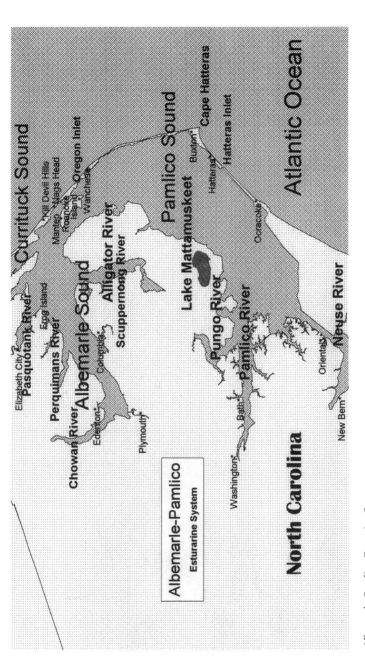

Albemarle-Pamlico Estuarine System

sand by the beginning of the eighteenth century, its depth changing
from around 16 feet to around 12 feet in the span of the previous thirty-
five years.

These two features of the waters west of the Outer Banks—their
shallowness and their shoals' tendencies to shift almost whimsically—
account for many of the watermen and boatbuilding traditions we find
on the coast today. Watermen need to be especially skilled at reading
the water's signs for hints of the structure of the bottom. An intimacy
with bottom formations is a prerequisite to understanding the habits of
fish and shellfish as well. Carolina watermen who grew up learning
about the estuary's bottom became indispensable to navigation and commerce during the early colonial period and later performed crucial tasks
of intelligence for fugitive slaves' escapes and during the Revolutionary
and Civil Wars.

Boats built around the sounds were uniquely designed to meet the
estuary's challenge. Flat-bottom barges towed haul seines out onto the
Chowan and Roanoke Rivers, encircling huge schools of herring and
shad. Wide-bodied tugs hauled timber floats from Plymouth to Elizabeth City, where they were towed up the Dismal Swamp Canal to Norfolk. A local design, the shad boat, sported a V-shaped, sweeping,
curving keel of juniper that rose to a wide hull, excellent for negotiating
rough waters near inlets on windy days. In some communities, boat
designs developed in concert with the deployment of new gear. South-
west of Cape Fear, off the Brunswick County coast, shrimp fishers and
boatbuilders built larger vessels to handle the drag of new, larger nets
that flared open by means of heavy wood doors.

Lined with several barrier islands, North Carolina's coast meets the
Atlantic sea traffic with fickle treachery while providing thousands of
protected, sheltered areas for fishing vessels and leisure craft. So many
shipwrecks lie just east of the barrier islands that the National Geographic Society publishes a map called "Ghost Fleet of the Outer
Banks," based on David Stick's wonderful thin volume *Graveyard of the
Atlantic*. These wrecks memorialize centuries of shipping, exploration,
and warfare. The oldest noted by Stick is the British Tiger, which sank

in 1585, but surely some older vessels piloted by Algonquins accompany the European wrecks. Inland, in Lake Phelps, dugout cypress canoes lie sunken, well preserved in the acidic water. The density of wrecks increases near the Oregon, Ocracoke, and Hatteras Inlets and just off Cape Hatteras, where the shoals constantly shift.

The barrier islands are only around 2,000 years old, formed as part of the changes in sea level and sedimentary deposits that occurred as the high-tide line moved back and forth more than 200 miles between ice ages. Some 17,000 years ago, at the height of the Ice Age, the coastline reached to what is today the edge of the continental shelf. Since that time, seacoasts around the world have been rising, creating an ever more scraggly coastline of spits and points, inlets and bays, islands, wetlands, and capes.

The legendary piracy, the Wright Brothers' first flight, and the Lost Colony lend the Outer Banks historical significance and romantic appeal, but the interior and southern sections of the coast are equally rich in tradition and legend. Blackbeard may have been killed at Ocracoke, but he made his home inland, in Bath, along the Pamlico River. Biologists know well the importance of the protected nursery areas of estuaries in the overall health of fish and shellfish populations, and hence in the health of the entire ocean. Largely separated from the ocean, North Carolina's rivers and sounds protect and sustain juvenile shellfish, fish, marine mammals and reptiles, and thousands of marine grasses and other plants. Microorganisms that resemble the heads of space aliens and benthic fauna that look like lice float around the sounds in the trillions. These feed in fresh and brackish waters.

Some species of microorganisms send terrifying signs and foretell alarming fortunes about the health of the estuaries. During certain episodes of oxygen depletion and conditions of deteriorating water quality, these microscopic beasts transform from plants into animals and become toxic, causing fish kills and neurological disorders in humans. In the early 1990s, several lab workers at North Carolina State University, working with high concentrations of a marine organism called a dinoflagellate, began suffering from memory loss, dizziness, nausea, and skin rashes. One marine biologist with a master of science degree dropped to an eighth-grade reading level from exposure. In García Márquez's *One Hundred Years of Solitude*, when the town of Macondo suffers a plague of insomnia and memory loss, citizens begin labeling their surroundings and describing the functions of things before their memories are lost forever: "Thus they went on living in a reality that was slipping away, momentarily captured by words, but which would escape irremediably when they forgot the values of the written letters."

Could there possibly be a more poignant symbol of negligence returning to haunt us than the almost science-fictional transformation of a benign plant into a poisonous animal capable of erasing human memory? Because there's the slightest chance it might succeed, I write this book.

NAMES
OF
WATER

"My name is Alice, but—"
"It's a stupid name enough!" Humpty Dumpty
interrupted impatiently. "What does it mean?"
"Must a name mean something?" Alice asked doubtfully.
"Of course it must," Humpty Dumpty said with a short laugh: "my
name means the shape I am—and a good handsome shape it is, too. With a
name like yours, you might be any shape, almost."
—Lewis Carroll, *Through the Looking Glass*

Too big a name will kill a small dog.
—Haitian Proverb

Pamlico. Neuse. Mattamuskeet. Chowan. How many of us think very deeply about the names of our surroundings? A well-known bit of anthropological trivia tells us that the Netsilik Eskimo have hundreds of names for the English-speaker's "snow." The different names derive from such characteristics as salt content, color, location, density, and use. By expanding the vocabulary of winter, we transform its character. We see not merely a Bing Crosby landscape or a frozen desert, but a new garden of possibilities. Early in the twentieth century, basing his conclusions on the accounts of travelers, merchants, and missionaries, George Fraser wrote in *The Golden Bough*:

> Primitive man regards his name as a vital portion of himself and guards it accordingly. . . . Blackfoot Indians believe that they would be unfortunate in all their undertakings if they were to speak their names. When the Canadian Indians were asked their names, they used to hang their heads in silence or answer that they did not know. . . . When the Nandi men are away on a foray, nobody at home may pronounce the names of the absent warriors; they must be referred to as birds. Should a child so far forget himself as to mention one of the distant ones by name, the mother would rebuke it, saying, "Don't talk of the birds who are in the heavens.". . . In primitive thought, the name of a person is not merely an appellation, but denotes what he is to the world outside himself—that is, his "outer" as distinguished from his "inner" being.

If names distinguish between the inner and outer beings, they also negotiate between them, drawing out the essential characters of things to present them as things human—things of use or beauty. Before the first Native Americans named parts of the Atlantic coastal plain, the estuaries, sounds, creeks, rivers, wetlands, and bays had no history, no biography. They had not been born in any human sense. Of course, they did exist, but when a tree falls in the forest and no one is around to hear it, does it matter to human history whether or not it makes a sound?

By naming parts of the coastal plain, the Carolina Algonquins and their predecessors launched their stewardship of water and land. The ways in which Algonquins named the waters and landmarks around them reflected their sense of the environment, their relationship to its

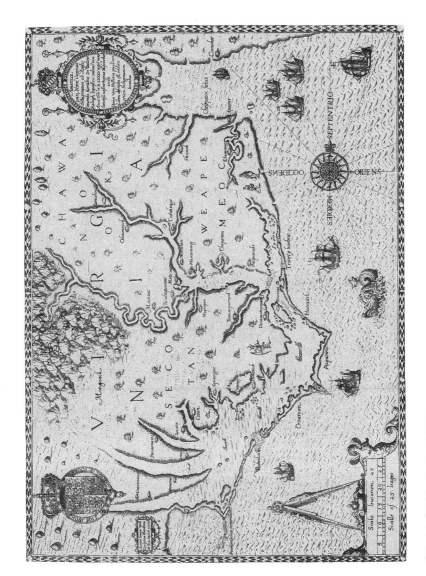

"Virginia," White-De Bry, 1590

gifts of shellfish, deer, acorns and hickory nuts, its medicinal flowers and herbs and edible roots. The quality and gravity of their naming, and the importance of the environment to their welfare, became intertwined. When the Algonquins named the lakes, rivers, and other parts of the estuary, the names they chose conveyed essential features of the waters themselves, or the place of water in group or community histories. Lake Mattamuskeet, the 30,000-acre lake in Hyde County that attracts thousands of swans and geese every winter, was originally indicated on European maps as Paquippe, which means "shallow lake." Later it was renamed Mattamuskeet, meaning "moving swamp" or "quaky bog." Both names derive from Algonquin phrases and words, but the designation changed between early and later maps. Maps produced during the sixteenth and seventeenth centuries used variations on "Paquippe," while later maps used Mattamuskeet.

Naming and portraying bodies of water was often a confused practice among early Europeans. Early mapmakers embellished maps of coastal waters of America with drawings of sea monsters that were almost mechanical in appearance, blowing smoke through dual exhaust pipes protruding from armored backs. Making the coast appear sinister may have fed early images of Native Americans as savage and barely human. It is likely, too, that European cartographers misunderstood Algonquin stewardship as much as Algonquins were confused about the motives of European mapmakers.

Long before the sixteenth century, maps were central to establishing legal control over property. Representing the surfaces of the earth and selecting names for towns, mountain ranges, wetlands, and other geographic features accompanied the drawing of borders and European claims on the North American continent. "Sometimes the process of mapping itself," writes Makower in his popular map catalog, "spurred the erosion of Indian land ownership." Early maps served strategic and military purposes, aiding in locating more and less defensible or vulnerable features of landscapes, and including data about the relative hostility of different groups or numbers of warriors. On maps, Europeans "showed the general locations of Indian tribes, bands, and villages, as well as the number of tents, lodges, and 'souls.' Later maps reflected the

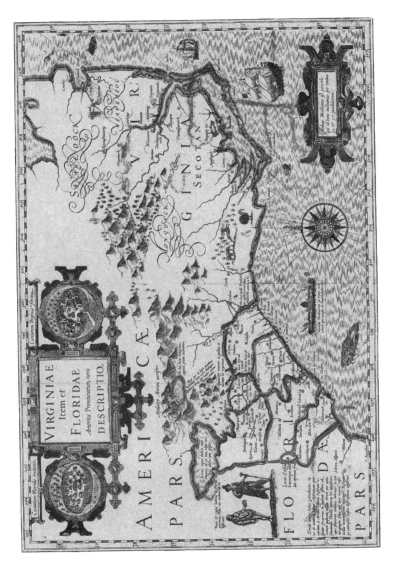

"Virginia and Florida," Mercator-Hondius, 1606

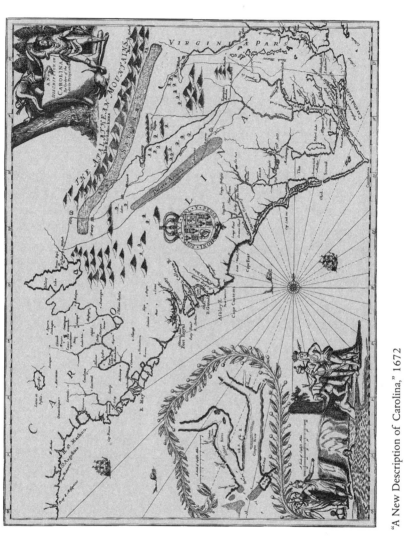

"A New Description of Carolina," 1672

growing conflict between Indians and whites: they stated numbers of warriors in a tribe, for instance, or the favorite haunts of raiding parties." Similar to the drawings of sea monsters, this emphasis on military matters often meant that the materials that survive about these early inhabitants portray them as overly aggressive and warlike. They dwell on population estimates and locations of settlements, reducing accounts of their lives to boring lists and geographical notations while gradually replacing the Algonquin names of water with their own surnames and imperial designations. By contrast, the Algonquin name for Mattamuskeet suggests other motives for naming water than either mapmaking or military conquest. Mattamuskeet *is* a shallow lake—only 5 feet deep at its deepest—and it does resemble a moving swamp, surrounded by wetlands that merge with its shoreline in reeds where the swans, mallards, wood ducks, and geese settle for the winter. It shimmers at its edges, where the reeds and rushes vibrate in even the most delicate of breezes, as though expanding its hold over the landscape.

Instead of appreciating its simplicity and beauty as a shallow body of water and feeding destination in the annual migrations of waterfowl, later Europeans made several attempts to drain the lake for farming. For nearly a century and a half, from 1789 to 1934, these efforts persisted without great success. Always the lake emerged the victor, thankfully not suffering the same fate as the once interconnected and haphazard waterways of Florida, where the wisdom of water control has been, quite recently, exposed as tomfoolery. Florida's Everglades are dying. Lake Okeechobee—a lake similar to Mattamuskeet in depth and other characteristics—has suffered health problems for decades. The word on Florida natives' lips to describe what is happening is "eutrophication." Simply, the waterways' diverse fishes and plants choke as fertilizers and cattle manure encourage overgrowths of oxygen-hungry grasses. Thankfully Mattamuskeet was designated a wildlife refuge before suffering a similar fate.

What do we know about the people who first encountered Lake Mattamuskeet? Humans first arrived along the eastern seaboard between 8,000 and 10,000 years ago, migrating east and south from ancestral populations of Canada. We know little about these people from the

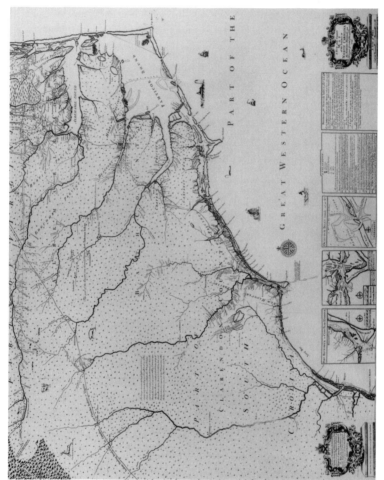

"Part of the Great Western Ocean," Moseley, 1733

materials they left us, but we can guess what they were like by piecing together a puzzle of geology, botany, linguistics, and contemporary ethnography. The key to this puzzle is archaeology. In eastern North Carolina, archaeologist David Phelps and his colleagues have drawn these fields of inquiry together to make sense of several excavations, including sites they speculated might have been the Algonquin village of Poemioc that several early European explorers mention in their journals and diaries.

Phelps conveys, in his lectures and writings, a sense of the constant change that occurs across coastal environments, daily by tides and minute by minute by wind and waves. "The Outer Banks," he writes, "are a fragile barrier constantly changing through time in response to the dynamics of nature, and their changing form in any synchronic segment along the time continuum is the result of a momentary balance between the dynamics of rising sea level, winds, storms, tides and sedimentary processes." From fifty years of archaeology, we have an accurate description of the sequence of the prehistoric occupation of the Mid-Atlantic coastal plain and the ways in which these early peoples dealt with their environments.

The phases of prehistoric occupation are the Paleo-Indian period (10,000 to 8,000 B.C.), the Archaic period (8,500 to 1,000 B.C.), and the three Woodland periods of Early (1,000 to 300 B.C.), Middle (300 B.C. to A.D. 800), and Late (A.D. 800 to A.D. 1584). Following these phases were roughly two centuries of slow genocide and disease called the Colonial period. By the 1790s there were virtually no viable indigenous villages left in the northeastern coastal regions, although several groups—the Meherrin, the Tuscarora, the Lumbee, the Pamunkey, and other groups—still exist in small pockets of ethnically self-conscious groups or inhabit tiny reservations north of Albemarle Sound in Virginia. Recently, there have been several attempts by these groups to achieve a new level of recognition by the federal government.

Archaeologists distinguish each of these phases by tool assemblages and the dietary stuff of trash heaps—primarily pieces of shell and bone and broken cooking vessels and other ceramics. They add this to information from ossuaries, other burials, and the artistic remains of decorations on pot shards or beads, comparing these, where relevant, to the material residues that result from living along the coast today. Much that we know about the original inhabitants of the coast—the Paleo-Indians—is speculative, partially because there may not have been many of them to leave much behind. "The scarcity of artifacts dating from this time period suggests Paleo-Indian population density was low," wrote Paul Gardner in a report about a site called Amity, east of Lake Mattamuskeet. Two of these original inhabitants dropped two fluted projectile points in what are today Tyrell County and Beaufort County. Most likely, the people of this period fastened these points to lances cut from trees like spruce, fir, juniper, or hickory. Along with lances, the coastal forests of this time provided hickory nuts, acorns, prickly pears, and persimmons, and sheltered raccoons, squirrels, rabbits, and deer. Often the handles of tools were more important to these people than the stone points and ax-heads they held, especially when their migrations carried them near significant sources of stone. Archaeologist Randy Daniel, describing prehistoric peoples living along river valleys stretching from the Neuse to the Oconee in Georgia, suggests that quarries of rhyolite, a particularly workable stone, focused groups into territories where chipping stone was less of a problem than carving wood.

Wood was, however, more readily available 8,000 years ago than today. In those days the coast was thickly wooded, similar to the boreal forests of northern Canada. Early peoples roamed through these forests in small bands of no more than thirty to fifty women, men, and children, following fresh water, fish, plants, and game supplies in seasonal migrations that were very likely circular or cyclical in nature. During brief yet exciting times of the year, food supplies may have been plentiful enough to aggregate large numbers of bands around sudden, if highly seasonal, volumes of food.

Weaving together archaeological and historical accounts, including oral history, Charles Heath traces the enduring importance of river herring in this regard, arguing that these fisheries served to aggregate people and provide crucial subsistence to peoples well into the twentieth century. Schools of river herring and shad, blackening the rivers and creeks during the late winter and spring, particularly during March and

April, brought together families that spread out thinly over the landscape during the rest of the year. Archaeologist John Byrd, digging along the Roanoke, at Jordan's Landing, listed herring and shad vertebrae among the most common bones found in trash heaps, implying a heavy reliance on these fishes for food. Both Byrd and Heath point out that the reliance on fish may have been much higher than the evidence suggests, because common sifting screens used in archaeological excavations are too wide to catch the tiny herring vertebrae.

Among prehistoric peoples, aggregation times—similar to the salmon runs of the Pacific Northwest, the piñon seasons of the Shoshoni, or the great whale migrations of the Netsilik—allowed young men and women to meet and talk with potential mates and allowed elders to trade information and goods, establish political alliances, and perform ceremonies that ensured the continuity of intertribal relations. These annual fairs are well documented in the literature on North American prehistory, and it is likely that they provided the basis for increased trade and settlement along the Atlantic Coast, influencing the founding and building of villages in the same way a city like St. Louis grew out of its strategic location at the confluence of the Missouri and Mississippi Rivers. State archaeologist Mark Mathis says that, before recent real-estate development, it would have been difficult to walk from South Carolina to Virginia without stepping on dozens of shell middens.

But interpreting the lives of the long dead is like reading in the shadows. Mistakes are common. Not everyone agrees about the exact nature of these early pioneers or the coastal landscape of 10,000 years ago. Some question the claim that the big firs and spruces of boreal forests actually swept from the Piedmont down the Atlantic slope. Whitehead's analysis of ancient pollen from Dismal Swamp suggests that boreal forest extended eastward from the hills at least to what is today Norfolk, but others argue that the boreal forest reached only to the Piedmont, after which it gave way to the scruffier pine forests we have on the coast today.

We do know that the coastline itself was quite different. Only 18,000 years ago the shore was several miles east of where it is today, reaching to the edge of the continental shelf. Neither the Chesapeake Bay nor the Pamlico Sound existed. Instead, the Susquehanna, the James, the Rappahannock, Albemarle, the Tar, the Pamlico, and other rivers cut deep ravines in the land and converged before reaching the Atlantic, emptying into the Hatteras Canyon, several miles off shore. Between 18,000 and 10,000 years ago, when the first humans arrived, the sea level was gradually creeping back, creating floodplains and bays.

At the confluence of rivers the potential existed for early humans to exploit fish and shellfish, but there were few stretches of shallow water, making marine resources less accessible than in later periods. Without protected and shallow areas, it would have been difficult to wade, launch fishing vessels, work nets or baskets, build fishing weirs, or gather aquatic animals and plants. At the same time, shallow water was and is necessary for sunlight penetration as well as other prerequisites of productivity. Juvenile fishes and crustaceans need places to hide, and the plants and animals at the base of the food chain need photosynthetic processes to reproduce and colonize an area. Early inhabitants of the Atlantic slope could not have relied heavily on aquatic resources until bays, islands, and estuaries began to form, as the sea levels continued rising. The first people along the Atlantic Coast, arriving midway between the end of the last ice age and the formation of the Outer Banks, pioneered and tested the cold waters of the coast during this period of estuarine formation. Gradually, over generations, as the coastline drew back, they brought more aquatic resources into their diets and their seasonal survival strategies.

It is doubtful that this happened at a constant rate. Human societies do not progress or decay with the precision of the half-lives of elements. If culture isn't broken we don't fix it—and often we don't fix it when it is. If contemporary and ethnohistorical accounts are any guides, the earliest arrivals reached this area through a long period of radiating into new areas because of seasonal movements combined with group fissioning and troubled relations with neighboring groups. Studies of contemporary hunting-and-gathering groups, combined with archaeological evidence, suggest that groups of early hunter-fisher-gatherers tended to break into two or more groups after they reached around forty individuals, although group sizes varied through the year and from place to place. Movements of game and the abundance of plant life—aspects of a territory's carrying capacity—encouraged this fissioning. As groups split, movement into new territories became inevitable. In the case of the migration from the Bering Strait into the eastern United States, this was a slow trek east and south. Between the first crossing of the Strait and the first human footstep in North Carolina, some 13,000 years elapsed. At five miles a day over 13,000 years, one could walk from Nome, Alaska, to Raleigh, North Carolina, more than 4,000 times. They weren't expanding their range at a pace of five miles a day, but at less than three miles a year.

Such a snail's pace allows plenty of time for reflection on one's environment. By what we know of today's hunting and gathering peoples, this is exactly what these early pioneers did. Moving into new ecological zones with the rules of thumb they possessed from their experiences in nearby, similar environments, they logged in accumulated memory the cues of plants, animals, winds, rains, sky, soil, and other components of the terrain. They paid attention to their surroundings with a scrutiny akin to the close examinations that led the Netsilik to coin so many names for "snow." We know this from current studies of people who depend heavily on natural cycles of fish and game and wild plant foods to survive. Indigenous botany and zoology—ethnobiology—are fields we are only now coming to appreciate. Only in the past few decades have anthropologists learned that people living directly off natural resources, particularly hunters, have ways to follow leads and act on hunches that are very similar to the methods Western science uses for experimentation. Indigenous peoples of the Americas developed several methods to make poisonous foods edible, often going through complex leaching and drying procedures that had to have taken years of trial and error to develop.

Other techniques enabled hunters to cope with stress and uncertainty as they migrated into unfamiliar territory. Scapulamancy, a hunting experimentation technique common among the Naskapi hunters of Labrador, consists of reading a caribou's collarbone after it has been charred and cracked by fire. Naskapi hunters will perform this ritual especially when they have not been having much luck with the hunt. The complete ritual involves taking steam baths, depriving oneself of sleep, and using other methods of achieving a dreamy or hallucinogenic state, tossing the caribou's scapula into the fire, and reading it as though it were a map of the surrounding forest: charred areas might indicate stands of trees or marshes, cracks might represent rivers, deeply burned areas might suggest a ridge or rocky slope, and so forth. The scapula-map also proposes directions in which to move to find caribou.

Seemingly senseless superstition, scapulamancy actually helps hunters succeed in their hunt by sending them in random directions after the caribou have learned to avoid their usual hunting grounds. It also helps the Naskapi reach a consensus about which way to go during a time when the stress of failure makes group decision-making difficult, focusing discussion about hunting strategy around the joint interpretation of the scapula. Scapulamancy achieves that balance between the hazards of discovery and the security of pooled, accumulated knowledge, which is very much like the way Western scientists practice their craft.

Like the Naskapi, it is likely that the Paleo-Indian groups along the Atlantic slope made decisions in light of the movements and habits of large animals, including a straight-horned species of bison that has since become extinct. This emphasis on big game—the defining feature of Paleo-Indian groups—made these early indigenous groups considerably different from the later Iroquoian, Siouan, and Algonquin groups that dominated North Carolina when the first Europeans landed. For the later groups, deer provided an important source of food, skins, and bone and antler tools, but it was one component of a much more varied and environmentally sensitive diet. Paleo-Indian groups, by contrast, relied on big-game hunting to the exclusion of hunting for many other plant and animal foods, having a less comprehensive and less intimate appreciation of their environment than later Native American groups. Many kill sites of the North American Paleo-Indian provide evidence of the crude and often wasteful way in which they dealt with nature. At one archaeologically famous site in Colorado, called Olsen-Chubbuck, archaeologists found evidence that Paleo-Indian hunters coordinated a stampede of more than 200 bison over a cliff, butchering some while leaving others untouched. Such crude methods may have hastened the extinction of mammoths, camels, horses, and other beasts during this time period. In several other ways Paleo-Indians differed from the Archaic and Woodland peoples. Paleo-Indians were constantly on the move, did not bury their dead in elaborate graves, developed no ceramics, and in the country that is today North Carolina and Virginia they occupied high ground much more than the coastal plain. From the hills, ridges, and mountains of the interior, from the banks of large rivers, they visited the coastal plain infrequently, and often merely to set up temporary camps for seasonally available foods. Paul Gardner speculates that Paleo-Indian groups might not have used the coastal plain because the rocks were not suitable for making projectile points, but David Phelps disputes this based on the wide variety of materials coastal peoples used to fashion their scrapers and points. At Paleo-Indian sites, Phelps has unearthed stone tools of quartz, quartzite, slate, ryolite, chert, and jasper. Bone tools were made from deer and fish, and wooden tools from oak, hickory, and hemlock. About the stone resources, Phelps writes: "In actuality, the eastern ridge of the Coastal Plain in Paleo-Indian times was 230 to 300 miles from the Piedmont, and all of the rivers with Mountain and Piedmont headwaters probably carried considerable loads of pebbles and cobbles downstream from their source."

The tools the Paleo-Indians made from these sources had to be big enough and heavy to penetrate thick hides and muscle tissue. They left behind spear points, primarily, but also knives, scrapers, atlatls (spear throwers), adzes, sickles, drills, and grinding stones. Undoubtedly they produced many more bone and wooden implements that have not survived to the present. Some fluted spear points—known as Clovis points—were as long as four or five inches and heavy, with a central groove for fitting onto a lance, but projectile-point manufacturing techniques were constantly being improved so that lumps of stone would yield ever more working edge.

Along the Atlantic slope the heavy emphasis on big game lasted around 2,000 years. In many eastern wooded areas, where large game animals had plenty of places to hide, early inhabitants were moving toward a broader diet earlier than Paleo-Indian peoples of the High

Plains. Very likely they mixed big-game hunting with collecting and hunting smaller mammals from seasonal campsites alongside the waterways, varying their diets with mussels and fish. "The subsistence strategy," writes Phelps, "may have been generalized hunting and gathering or may have emphasized the hunting of larger animals as in the classic model, although a combination of these strategies seems most plausible."

Why would Phelps suspect the coastal Paleo-Indians of breaking with the classic big-game tradition? Because the swelling and joining of rivers that occurred in coastal North Carolina 10,000 years ago encouraged alternative lifestyles that were more attached to water. Water collects, transports, and deposits stones, seeds, bones, and wooden objects useful for tool manufacture, while providing fertile shorelines and fairly accessible resources of fish and shellfish, turtles, frogs, muskrats, and other small mammals. Most early civilizations and ancient cities developed on or near important river systems: the Tigress and the Euphrates in the Middle East, the Nile in Egypt, the Yang Tze and Huang Ho in China. In North America the Mississippi and Ohio River valleys supported the Hopewell and other mound-builders. In like fashion the coastal plain of eastern North Carolina and Virginia attracted more and more peoples and encouraged the development of better technologies and more complex political and social organizations.

During the Archaic period, beginning around 8,000 years ago, social and technical developments occurred along with changing plant and animal communities. Oak and hickory forests gradually overtook the pine-hemlock-birch forests of the previous two millenniums, and by 6,000 B.C. the flora and fauna we encounter today were taking root. Remember that the seacoasts were still farther east of today's coastline and that the formation of the Outer Banks was still 4,000 years away. Even without the contemporary beauty of these big endearing sandbars, migration to the coast was heavy during the Archaic period. Quite suddenly, advanced projectile points from the Piedmont and the mountains appear, signs of people coming from the west and north and setting up seasonal camps and permanent settlements. At the seasonal camps, they brought with them their less elaborate ceramic vessels the same way we, as tourists renting beach houses, might bring our cheaper dishes and utensils and leave the good china and silver at home.

The seasonal hunting tradition established by these nameless early peoples lasted until well into the twentieth century: photographs from the first decades of this century captured men in split-wood hunting and fishing shacks along the Outer Banks, showing off stringers of wood ducks or mallards. Out of these seasonal excursions grew the tradition of carving duck, goose, and swan decoys, and waterfowl hunting clubs are almost as numerous as shipwrecks along the North Carolina coast. A local oral historian named Captain Jim tells stories about the loon-eating Ca'e Bankers—those who roamed freely along the Outer Banks before they were forced into settlements by hurricanes and legal judgments. In the summertime, they hosted parties where they would use up an entire box of shotgun shells just to shoot and eat a single loon, obviously not depending on these low-flying, diving birds as a main food source.

Archaic peoples could not have known they were beginning a tradition of seasonal occupation of the coast that was to last 8,000 years, but their migrations suggest they recognized the advantages of water. Slowly, over the next 4,000 years, they established settlements in the coastal zone. Almost exclusively, they chose sites close to rivers and streams instead of upland areas. The largest of camps occurred at the confluence of large streams. With river's edge settlement, Archaic peoples flourished technically and culturally. Round, grooved balls served as weights on spear throwers or atlatls, achieving far greater distance and accuracy. Ceramics hardened. Weaving tightened. Trade blossomed. Boatbuilding progressed. By 2,000 B.C. these people were burying their dead in elaborate mounds, sailing across the sounds in canoes that could carry twenty or more men, and stitching clothing with delicate bone needles. They were becoming at once capable of monumental feats requiring political organization and leadership while honing the skill necessary to refine tiny objects into finer, more effective tools. Delicacy and grace accompanied glory and bravado.

In the David Phelps Archaeology Lab at East Carolina University, the material remains of these achievements are bagged, tagged, numbered, and reassembled. Prehistory's residues crowd every desktop and table surface, organized into trays representing segments of sites and shelves showing transitions from straight to curved-lipped vessels. Other displays show the progress from long, heavy spear points to the half-inch quartz triangular arrowheads of the Woodland period, some so light you wouldn't think them any more capable of felling game than a single ball of buckshot. Artifacts recovered from this time period show the emergence of regional and perhaps ethnic differences, laying the groundwork for later hostilities among the tribes. Gradually the Neuse River system emerged as a rough border between Northern and Southern cultural traditions. Ceramic styles and firing techniques developed on either side of the Neuse begin to differ during this period, reflecting different technological influences and different artistic traditions. Around this same time we see that only the people of the southern and western coastal plain bury their dead in mounds, while people north and east of the Neuse continued burying their dead in simple, humble graves. The ethnic diversity encountered by early Europeans along the Mid-Atlantic Coast, however, makes sweeping generalizations suspect.

The Neuse's boundary between north and south marks a significant break for the entire eastern seaboard, as though this river were mimicking Cape Hatteras's natural boundary between many northern and southern species of fish. Northeastern North Carolina constitutes the southernmost territory of the Algonquin-speaking peoples, who extended from the Neuse River into the Great Lakes and Canada, while southeastern North Carolina marks the northernmost territory of the Siouan peoples, whose affiliated ethnic groups reached southward through South Carolina and across the Savannah River into Georgia. To the immediate west of these two groups, along a line extending north-south across the main watersheds of the coastal plain, lived the Tuscarora, an Iroquoian-speaking people who waged war against the British and their Native American allies from 1711 to 1713. Early Europeans described them as "powerful and addicted to trade," and the Tuscarora demand the dignity of some digression on their historical trajectory and their real and symbolic importance in North Carolina.

The Tuscarora were and are important to North Carolina's coastal peoples because people calling themselves Tuscarora survive today in parts of the southeastern coastal plain and along the northern narrows of the Chowan River. Their ability to adapt and their taste for struggle may have been responsible for their endurance. Today they continue fighting, engaged in a prolonged legal battle for recognition from the Bureau of Indian Affairs. As recently as 1987 this struggle erupted into violence when two Tuscarora men held Robeson County's principal newspaper's staff hostage for about seventy-two hours, protesting abusive conditions in the county jail, the murder of a young African-American man by the sheriff's son, and the lack of federal recognition of North Carolina Lumbee and Tuscarora.

At Somerset Plantation, near the shores of Lake Phelps, on a rainy Sunday in June I heard a story about a Tuscarora man that derived from an archaeologist's encounter with something personal the man left behind. The fact that I had been reading about coastal Native Americans helped, providing the background that, partially imagined, is what it takes sometimes to approach cultural understanding. I had been wandering through several articles and books on the tribes of the Southeast and the East, catching a glimpse here and there of what it must have been like, smelling wood smoke in the distance or hearing a shaman's chant or a priest's blessing. I had grown all too familiar with John White's drawings, Maurice Mook's speculative histories of settlement, and the capsule descriptions and population estimates of Swanton. But until that Sunday I had no feel for the people, no sense of their experience.

What happened was quite simple: David Phelps described the contents of a cloth purse recovered from excavations at Neoherooka, the Tuscarora Fort near Snow Hill, and I connected with the description the way you connect with an utterance you consider true. It sent a chill through me. It may have been the setting, the historical importance of Lake Phelps, which still preserves ancient Indian canoes, or Somerset

Plantation, where slaves, fresh from Africa and considered too wild for any measure of freedom, were forced to dig irrigation canals while still inside their cages.

Phelps speculated that the man carrying the purse into the fort fully expected to leave with the purse in his possession, for among the personal items were squash seeds and kernels of corn for the next season's planting. Two clay pipes, a handful of tobacco, musketballs for killing humans and buckshot for deer, firing flints, and glass beads constituted the rest of the purse's contents—items at once utilitarian and personal. Though these were simple, everyday things to the Tuscarora, Phelps spoke of them as though they were the talismans of a holy man. And I prefer to believe that during the purse owner's last moments, when the Tuscarora's loss was imminent, he drew some small comfort from having his things beside him, feeling the purse's contents as a nun might run a rosary through her fingers, remembering how he came by each of the possessions, each of these common warrior's things. Imagining this process of acquisition is often all that archaeological and ethnohistorical accounts allow. For most of his life, it is likely that the warrior loved trading, like most Tuscarora, because trade took him into new territories among the Algonquin peoples living along the waters to the east in dispersed wigwams, just inside Secotan territory.

Any trading with coastal peoples would have been most productive during herring season. Archaeologists argue that herring resources began contributing to increases in settlement and regional population increases as early as 3,000 years ago. Herring are particularly easy to preserve by smoking, a process that John White recorded in his drawings of Algonquins. Along with smoked fish, the coastal groups traded marginella shells for smooth pipes made of the fine clays of the foothills.

Among the villages visited by the Tuscarora traders was the large, well-known town of Poemioc, depicted near Lake Mattamuskeet on early maps. In Poemioc, the royal dead lay on mortuary scaffolds until the priests stripped the skin from their bones, in preparation for their burial. From White's paintings we know that around the cluster of wigwams was a palisade of poles that overlapped at the village gate. In the center of the village burned an eternal fire, where a huge clay vat of

Algonquins building a canoe, John White painting, c. 1580

Algonquins fishing, John White painting, c. 1580

Algonquins smoking fish, John White painting, c. 1580

soup boiled endlessly. They received guests in the longhouse, parting woven mats of black needlerush marsh grass and inviting them to sit around a fire in the center of the floor. As if that was not smoky enough, Native Americans typically lit pipes and exchanged tobacco as token trades, priming the artesian wells of commerce.

In and around coastal villages, news of a visitor's arrival traveled through the networks of kinfolk, families organized around the bloodlines of fathers and mothers, for among common people any goods a man acquired through trade he divided among his children and wives. Only the titles and honors of royalty were passed exclusively through female kin, which was why the great chief Powhatan, to the north, was succeeded by his second brother, Opechancanough, instead of his son.

By the sixteenth century, it was likely that most peoples along the coast had heard of Powhatan's thirty tribes, the largest confederacy of the rivers and bays, stretching from the northern tip of the Chesapeake south into Meherrin territory, around Albemarle. Many of the coastal groups, such as the Secotan, were less tightly tied into tribute systems, freer to engage in trade on their own behalf. Powhatan inherited only six tribes, but passed thirty to Opechancanough from his skill as a military leader. He crafted victory from treachery as often as from military might. In this way he built the fragile confederacy that the English whittled away from within. Opechancanough died after internal strife, and the last emperor, a Pamunkey Queen, placed in power with English assistance, was so weak she could not collect tribute from many of the peoples Powhatan ruled.

Knowledge of political developments passed from longhouse to longhouse and from village to village through oral history and commentary, the signature of the elders, whether Secotan or Chowanoc or Tuscarora. They baptized the waters and lands with origin myths and descriptive appellations.

They were too kind to the Europeans. The earliest encounters were classic misunderstandings. In one account, a sailor whose vessel capsized was helped ashore by a group of Algonquins near Cape Hatteras. When they built a fire, the sailor, perhaps remembering Columbus's exaggerated accounts of cannibals in the Caribbean, assumed they were going to roast him, but instead they dried his clothes over the flames, righted his vessel, filled it with fish, and sent him back to his mother ship. Later, when the English arrived, the Algonquin groups taught them how to fasten the spines of horseshoe crabs to spears and night fish, blinding fish with fires built inside canoes or with handheld torches along the bank. They taught them how to build weirs along the rivers, how to trap sturgeon in the shallows, how to dip baskets and nets into the boil of herring during late winter and spring. Oral histories from this time period suggest that the Secotan, Chowanoc, Croatan, and other coastal peoples considered the English a stupid and smelly people. The English stewed in their own sweat and built thick-walled houses out of trees older than the thin saplings the Indians used for longhouses and wigwams. By contrast, Native American women built their houses in much the same way they raised a child, using materials from nearby the village. The men hunted and traded corn for glass beads, peaches for textiles, and deer skins for brass kettles, which they cut up for knives and arrowheads.

This was before they traded gunfire. The warrior whose purse David Phelps discovered years after the battle at Neoherooka, in the last moments of his life, must have felt particularly betrayed. It was the trade in goods, primarily deer skins, that led to many of the problems with Europeans. Eric Wolf's monumental *Europe and the People Without History*, in a chapter on the North American fur trade, demonstrates how trade in beaver pelts and other skins, usually for firearms, fostered shifts in the balance of powers among the tribes as different groups tried to establish control over the trade. The shift from trade resembling gift exchange to the commerce of violence stemmed from the old misunderstandings and the desires of the English to rope off and possess the new continent for its own use. In this endeavor they recruited Yamassee warriors from what is today South Carolina. In one well-known early incident, the English burned a village called Aquascogoc and all its cornfields over a missing silver cup, meting out a particularly harsh, exemplary punishment for what was likely a single individual's infraction.

These punishments persisted and even worsened. Burning cornfields, like killing off the bison on the Great Plains, was a way of weakening groups that failed to comply with English demands, customs, or desires, even when those failures of compliance were due more to cultural misunderstandings than to actual ill will. Combined with the slower yet more devastating deaths from European disease, against which even the healthiest Algonquins had no immunities, the end of 10,000 years of Indian occupation of eastern Virginia and North Carolina occurred over seven or eight generations. There was not even time to record their knowledge of the medicinal values of animals, fish, and plants, let alone reconstruct the detailed paths by which they traveled from loose bands of hunters and gatherers to the confederacies and well-fed people encountered by John White.

Algonquin peoples left us plenty of buried material remains, yet few aspects of their thought remain beyond what we can glean from how they named their surroundings. We do not know whether or not Algonquins treated names as inalienable—that is, as things that are so closely united with individuals and with things that they acquire the same sacred sense we associate with heirlooms. From Fraser's *Golden Bough*, quoted earlier, as well as from other anthropological sources, we know that many Native American groups considered names more tangible and less interchangeable than we tend to consider them. At the death of his brother, the famous Algonquin Werowance Wingina changed his name to Pemisapan, suggesting that names were intimately bound with states of being among relatives or, at the very least, that they possessed a significance that differs from the significance names have for us. A reverence for names and naming is not unique to Native Americans. Bushmen of the Kalahari Desert, in southern Africa, possess a finite number of names. Selecting a name involves remembering past individuals who were called by the same name—that is, it involves remembering the history of the Bushmen. Among people with no written language, such oral traditions become central to identity. When we repeat Algonquin names of bodies of water, it is likely we are recalling elements of their remembering, of their history.

As with their keen observations of Mattamuskeet, Algonquin names reveal the ways these early inhabitants thought about land and water. "Hatteras," for example, an open space of short bushy covering, derives from an Algonquin expression meaning "there is less vegetation." "Pasquotank" derives from the Algonquin phrase meaning "where the current divides." And "Chowan" derives from the name of a people who called themselves *and* their territory the Chowanoc. The ways Algonquin groups named water and land either described features of the landscape or tied groups of people to territories by common names. Their names of water reflected not only their respect for and stewardship of the water, but also that that stewardship was embedded in a common heritage and ancestry.

By contrast, many of the European names of water derived from the names of individuals rather than entire groups or clans of people, reflecting European mapmaking traditions and the European notion that individuals could own the land and water. Albemarle, for example, was named for George Monck, Duke of Albemarle, and Beaufort was named for Henry Somerset, Duke of Beaufort. Beaufort was built on the site of an Indian town called Wareiock, which meant "fishing village." Ironically, Europeans sometimes even named places after individuals when they used Indian words and names on their maps and records, as in the cases of Wanchese and Manteo.

Not all European place names reflected the sense of individual ownership. Many European names of the Mid-Atlantic Coast describe the places they name—Swan Quarter, Broad Creek, Cedar Island, Piney Point—and others reflect common traditions and group identities, such as New Bern, Plymouth, New Hanover, and Carolina Beach, or common histories even when they are named after individuals, such as Washington or Jacksonville. Still, the European colonization of the Mid-Atlantic Coast ushered in a shift from stewardship and community ownership of land and water to one of privatization and individual ownership—two different means of engaging in dialogues and exchanges with the coastal resources, two separate paths of development. In the struggle between them, the history of the Mid-Atlantic Coast has been written ever since.

EARLY
FISHERIES,
OILY
FISHERIES

Easter Monday. In Jamesville, on the Roanoke, the cooks rise early to arrange the supplies of rockfish, herring, and perch in the coolers in restaurants along the south shore of the river. Upstream and down, men in small boats drift with gill nets as fishermen have since the second week of January. Ray Thomas began his set at the mouth of Broad Creek. At Jamesville he lifts his 75-foot net, across from the Cypress Grill, checking the catch by flashlight. Years ago, a set like this would yield 600 or 700 herring, but this morning they raise from the brown water fewer than 100 of the blue-and-silver fish. The oldest inhabitants of Jamesville remember Aprils that the Roanoke and Chowan Rivers turned black with herring and shad. The seines they used then tickled the bottom, occasionally netting a sturgeon, that big primitive fish with the look of the Late Cretaceous. But the same runoffs into the rivers, the same dams that are killing the herring, have all but erased sturgeon from the Roanoke.

With the morning light comes the first frying of herring of the day, the cooks testing the heat of the corn oil. The familiar scent diffuses through Jamesville and meanders out as far as the highway that will bring folk from Williamston and Plymouth into town for the festival and the feast. Downriver, as the first of the boats prepare to land their catch, Dixie Blue lights the heater in a fish shack and arranges her buckets along the cutting line—one for fish, one for heads and guts, one for the lovely orange roe. Around the blue flame of the heater her seven co-workers gather, waiting to cut fish for families that are just now waking to the demands of the youngest of their children. Thirty miles away, up the Chowan, the women at Perry-Wynn Fishery in Colerain wait for the first of the herring boats, as eager as Dixie to finish cutting and join the day's festivities. Since the eighteenth century, families have come to watch the catch the day after Easter, bringing their own barrels, their own salt, buying cut fish directly from the fisheries.

By noon Jamesville's streets are lined with cars and all the restaurants serving herring have waiting-lines for the crispy fish. Local vinegars and hot sauces crowd around napkin dispensers for seasoning coleslaw, hush puppies, stewed potatoes and creamed corn served with the once prolific fish. Now more than half the herring served through the Easter season come from other waters, other states, although everywhere the catches are falling as engineers extend the jetties, dredge, fill, dam, and channel, ruining the water's wayward ways.

Dixie finishes a half day's work on the catch, which only a few years earlier would have taken her well into the evening. Downstream, Ray turns toward shore, rolls up his net, and locks it away in his fisherman's shack on the water. The season's over. The fishery's dying. For the first time in his life he believes that the poet who, for so many generations, couldn't have been more wrong, finally, now, was right when he said, "April is the cruelest month."

Early European fisheries along the Outer Banks and inside Albemarle, Pamlico, and neighboring waters began at two distinct social locations: at the heart of the plantation system and on the fringes of colonial power. Fisheries that operated from inside the plantation system mobilized hundreds of women and men every spring to operate haul seines and land, cut, salt, and pack upward of 250,000 pounds of river herring and shad a day.

Those on the edge of colonial power, close to the frontier, were far more passive. They began as families along the Outer Banks happened on beached whales and porpoises and rendered or "tried out" their oil on brick stoves. Theirs was a household economy whose members sold fish and oil as part of a diverse survival strategy of fishing, trapping, hunting, and part-time, casual work in towns and on plantations. The others, the slaveholding planters who organized the big herring and shad fisheries, were deeply embedded in an economic system designed to produce for export, for trade. Along with salted fish, they shipped tobacco, cotton, wheat, and corn across Albemarle Sound to Elizabeth City, up the Dismal Swamp Canal, across the Chesapeake, and north to Baltimore, where it was rerouted to Europe and into the southern holdings of the British Empire. Their corned herring fed planters and slaves throughout the U.S. South and the English Colonies of the West Indies.

From these two social locations came two different fishing traditions: the one large, requiring centralized coordination, large numbers of enslaved, indentured, and hired workers, and an almost factory-like regimen; the other small, diverse, and food-producing, seated in family, worked by fathers and sons on the water and mothers and daughters on shore. Both the herring fishery and whaling were tied into markets for fish and fisheries products, but the motives of their practitioners were vastly different. They established an early distinction between big, capital-intensive enterprises and small, family-organized fishing operations, a distinction we still see today when we compare the factory-organized menhaden fleets with the thousands of crabbers' families soaking pots in the rivers, creeks, and sounds.

Supplementing plantation agriculture, the herring and shad fisheries used the same workers—slaves, indentured servants, and free men—who felled trees, cleared fields, dug canals for drainage, irrigation, and transport, and tended cotton, corn, wheat, tobacco, and livestock. Mark Taylor, in his work on seiners and tongers in early North Carolina fisheries, describes Alexander Brownrigg's fishery on the Chowan as consisting of a 1,020-foot seine operated by a winch on shore, capable of catching more than 100,000 herring in two days of fishing. During the heavy herring runs, when the rivers boiled with fish, these fisheries operated around the clock.

The most productive early herring fisheries were founded in the early eighteenth century on rivers emptying into the western and northern waters of Albemarle Sound, relying on the port cities of Elizabeth City, Edenton, and Plymouth. Operations located along the Chowan and Roanoke Rivers are the best known, but herring and shad spawn in all the tributaries of Albemarle and the Chesapeake Bay. These later fisheries built on and capitalized on earlier traditions. Algonquin and Iroquois groups dipped nets and baskets into shallow creeks to catch these fish; later settlers, many of them European indentured servants who satisfied their contracts and established small farms along the sound, fashioned long-handled dip nets to fish these same finger streams emptying into Albemarle. A later manifestation of the dip net—chickenwire molded into a bowl shape and lashed to a pole—inspired what people along the Roanoke, between Jamesville and Plymouth, called a "fishing machine": a conveyor belt of mesh basket scoops that dipped into the river and flipped herring into wooden barges. During some herring runs these machines, left unattended too long, would sink under the weight of the catch.

Outside of dip-netting herring, proprietors of large fisheries of the eighteenth and nineteenth centuries restricted the use of any nets besides their own haul seines in the choicest river locations. They were able to gain monopolistic control over these waters because of their ties to power. Links between early planters and seats of colonial power were tight. Among early powerful landowners of the Albemarle region were eight men—the Lords Proprietors—whom King Charles II himself rewarded for political support during the royal family's exile and fight to reestablish the monarchy in England. Surviving paintings of men of this rank show off their court manners and fine clothing, disguising military and in some cases heroic backgrounds. Yet by the time they became Lords over land grants in the New World, they were beyond personal adventure.

When George Monck, the Duke of Albemarle, became a Proprietor, he was baby-faced and fat, sporting thick eyebrows and a thin mustache; in a well-known painting he is dressed up in satin sashes and ruffles and carries a gentleman's walking stick. He looks to be around forty-five years old, or about the age when he assumed a position in the House of Commons. From the look of him—well-fed, well-dressed, serious, contemplative, arrogant—one would never guess that he had commanded a regiment in Dublin during the Irish rebellion, joined Cromwell's invasion of Scotland, or led battles against the Dutch. Perhaps early victories allowed him to recline in the fame of his achievements. Land grants to men like Monck were preceded by Queen Elizabeth's grants to Sir Humphrey Gilbert and his half-brother, Walter Raleigh, and Charles I's grant to Sir Robert Heath—all of whom relied on emissaries, who in turn relied on other emissaries, to settle the Americas. It is no mere coincidence that Shakespeare's parody of early attempts at settlement, *The Tempest*, is a tragic comedy; most of what we know about the early expeditions is a blend of tragedy and comedy.

As adventurers pioneering and establishing settlements, men like Philip Amadas, Arthur Barlowe, and John White bungled several attempts to gain a foothold on North America's Atlantic coasts. The Lost Colony was only one of several well-financed failures, its misplaced inhabitants most likely welcomed and eventually absorbed by the more knowledgeable, better adapted Croatan people, from whose perspective British customs and survival practices appeared quite foolish. Helen Roundtree, writing about the slow pace of change among the Pamunkey of southern Virginia, says that change came slowly to these peoples in part because the Pamunkey thought many of the European practices were ridiculous. The Pamunkey considered the houses of the English particularly stupid. Log cabins were not much warmer than native wigwams in the winter, were far too labor-intensive and permanent, and were much more oppressive during the summer.

While White and Barlowe spread stories around Europe of the New World, many of them fictional, bringing Wanchese and Manteo to parties and inspiring Shakespeare to write *The Tempest*, it took the anonymous, solitary, less venerated hunters, fishers, trappers, and fur and deerskin traders to trickle out of Jamestown and settle the Mid-Atlantic coastal plain. Through the first half of the seventeenth century, they cut paths and homesteads into the cypress and pine forests north of Albe-marle and along the Chowan, Pasquotank, and Perquimmans Rivers, which the spring herring runs blackened with their spawning.

It was only after successful settlement by a handful of European colo-nists—around 500 by the mid-1600s—that more powerful landowners established larger plantations, financing cotton, wheat, and tobacco farming and initiating the plantation agriculture that would eventually branch out into herring fishing. Some of these ventures were substantial, yet the area between Jamestown and the north shore of Albemarle Sound never saw the growth of the huge slave plantations that define much of the South in the American imagination. Early settlers did own slaves and plant crops for international trade, but the intricate, shallow, and treacherous waterways inhibited plantation development. The notable exception, Somerset, on the shores of Lake Phelps, kept its original African slaves in cages while they dug the drainage canals, suggesting great difficulty establishing authoritarian control over large numbers of slaves in a swampy frontier. Later, during the Civil War, Somerset's owner complained that the slaves virtually assumed control of the plan-tation, and today the site witnesses an annual reunion for the descen-dants of these rebellious slaves, celebrating this local flowering of African-American resistance. Dorothy Redford, the author of the princi-pal book about Somerset and today's manager of the historic site, em-bodies this assertiveness. She descended from the same slaves who irrigated the fields through cage bars, and her deep, rich voice reaches into the history of the place. She claims to know the ghosts who haunt the grounds as intimately as the centuries-old recipes for corn bread. She dips candles, makes brooms, spins cotton. She is a dominating figure, confident, poised, intelligent, a living testament to the enduring head-strong spirit of the region's original West Africans.

The wilderness between plantations and towns around Albemarle en-couraged resistance against organized European powers. The bars of Somerset's slave cages may have been the most extreme form of popula-tion control, but many early Carolinians struggled against planters, mer-chants, and other colonial powers who kept them in debt and bound them with contracts of indenture and other obligations to the British Empire. Intricate legal and informal relations of servitude and authority permeated the Albemarle region, stimulating an equally intricate network of clandestine relations among fugitive slaves, Indians, pirates, watermen, small independent farmers, hunters, swamp dwellers, trappers, and assorted drifters. As David Cecelski notes in his fine work on the underground railroad, the illegal and rebellious nature of the activities of these individuals, combined with reduced access to literacy, demands that much of this history be pieced together in the few biographies that exist and in how the official concerns of the powerful reflect threats to their power. In the mists and shadows of these accounts, we can perceive the most tenuous of links between the huge plantation fisheries and the frontier households that founded the family fisheries that rendered oil from whales on the Outer Banks.

Herring and shad fisheries were springtime operations. Beginning in late January and lasting through Easter, fishing peaked for six to eight weeks through March and April. During this time, these fisheries were as voracious as hungry bluefish in their consumption of labor power and materials. Each fishery required between forty and eighty workers to set and haul the seines and to cut, salt, and pack the fish in barrels. Mules, horses, and men powered the windlasses that hauled in the seines. Sometimes as many as sixteen to eighteen draught animals worked each seine. Some of the early seines were 8,000 feet long and 18 feet deep, lined with cork floats on top and weights below.

A typical operation along North Carolina's Albemarle Sound, described in *Harper's New Monthly Magazine* in 1857, illustrates the scope of the fisheries that developed along the Mid-Atlantic coast during the first 200 years of European settlement. Two barges, each carrying half the seine and powered by up to ten oarsmen, would move out from shore, side by side, to a predesignated point in the river. There they would part, one turning upstream and one down, playing out the seine. Finishing, they brought the two ends to the beach and fastened two primary

Fishers seining on the Albemarle Sound, c. 1900

lines to the mule-driven windlasses and several smaller lines to points along the riverbank to maintain the seine's shape as they hauled it in.

As the net tightened, the herring began to boil. Sea birds flocked over the catch. Gulls, ospreys, and eagles circled and dove to snag fish. The commotion of fish and birds and the excitement of the catch electrified the shoreline. Men scurried back and forth along the bank, tending to the shape and integrity of the net, pulling ropes, whipping horses and mules, and preparing for the last haul onto the beach and division of the catch into herring, shad, and by-catch. Women sharpened knives and arranged wooden buckets along the beach, waiting on short stools, smoking pipefuls of rope tobacco sold in slave markets. Families collected along the fringes of the fishing: ladies from Edenton, house servants from Colerain, trappers and woodsmen from deep inside the wild

Men pulling a seine over the battery, Jamesville, North Carolina, c. 1920

Carolina bush. The aerosol spray of thousands of fins misted everyone with the river's smell.

People came to buy whole shad or barrels of salted herring, or came prepared to cut, salt, and pack the fish themselves. In the seines, along with the herring and shad, were striped bass, perch, gray trout, mullet, gar, sturgeon. Eels and lampreys wiggled in the mass. Whiskered and flat fishes, fish that stung, fish with poisonous spines, fish named for choking swine, and fish whose open mouths housed white bugs with black eyes all spilled from the net. Once landed, the rush of thousands of fins and flapping fish bodies sounded like the trade winds forcing sand through yaupon trees.

Quickly the men shored up the net with boards, erecting a makeshift wooden wall between the beach and the river. Moving in on the catch, they separated the highly valued shad and shoveled the herring and other fish into buckets for the cutters and packers. Most cutters were women. One widely reprinted drawing shows a group of six black women cutting the heads off herring on boards balanced across the lips of wooden buckets. In the foreground a large middle-aged black woman wearing a bonnet and smoking a long-stemmed corncob pipe poises a butcher knife above a herring. A rope handle dangles from her bucket.

Cleaning a haul of fish, Avoca, North Carolina, c. 1900

Her hands and forearms look strong and muscled; probably the hands are callused, for she wears no gloves. A scarf and apron serve as her only protective gear. Fish resembling pinfish or brim, a single eel, and big striped bass litter the ground around her work.

These women earned 50 cents a day, a barrel of salted herring, and what labor recruiters of the day called "offal"—fish considered scrap or by-catch, some of which were fish we prize highly today. One day in April, more than 130 years after *Harper's* published the drawing of black women deheading herring, I visited a small cutting house on the Cho-

Women cleaning herring, Edenton, North Carolina, c. 1920

wan River, just outside Colerain. It was located, quite literally, on the water: a boardwalk crossed a stretch of wetlands to the fish house door, beside which sat a yellow cylinder with raised metal interior cleats that, when rotated, scraped silvery scales off herring. Inside were eight black women making quick cuts across the herring, separating the head from the body and, with a skillful twist of the knife, cutting along the length of the fish's belly, gutting the fish at the same time. This task has not changed appreciably in 350 years. Then as now, a skilled cutter could head, gut, pack, and salt between 4,000 and 6,000 herring on a day of steady, seemingly endless supply.

These women and the hired hands working the mules and the nets, many sleeping at the fishery's dormitories, rounded out household incomes that drew on several of the coast's opportunities. Planters' men recruited seasonal workers up and down the Chowan and Albemarle, sending out word that reached into the hidden cabins of woodsmen, through lively fishermen's courts along the water, and as far as camps of fugitive slaves cutting cypress shingles in the Great Dismal Swamp. These networks of recruiters and workers, of families buying salted fish for the winter, of the earliest of watermen and slaves still at large from Carolina and Virginia planters, constituted a cross section of coastal society, every March and April, at nearly any point between the middle of the eighteenth century and the Civil War. Even today the big fisheries at Colerain and Edenton reach into households for workers who rely on several other jobs and income sources to survive. Even today the landing of herring at the fisheries, at Easter, lures families from dozens of coastal cities and small towns to the spectacle. Even today these are lively, festive, at times breathless assemblages of people and skills and fish.

Anyone who has ever attended a high school football or basketball game is familiar with assemblies similar to this. I remember reading Julian Steward's work on the Shoshone and Paiute of the Great Basin and thinking how spectacular it must have been during piñon nut season, when families came in from the reaches of the desert, on foot or horseback, with infants and old people, middle-aged hunters and women whose sharp sense of smell could locate a roadrunner's nest at the base of a cactus across a wide arroyo. During most of the year, they remained dispersed over the dry, harsh landscape, in small bands of fifteen to twenty-five, gleaning sparse fruits from the Mohave, the Bonneville Salt Flats, the Painted Desert. But when the pine trees bore their fruits everyone came together, suddenly yet seasonally, hundreds of families with the news and experience of millions of grains of sand spread over thousands of miles, the trees plentiful, water flowing, the game fat and lazy. During these big seasonal assemblages they arranged marriages, exchanged folk tales, danced, sang, traded, formed alliances, cemented loyalties.

Gatherings like this pepper our lives the same way momentous events pepper our histories—the Wright brothers' flight, the sit-in at the Woolworth's lunch counter, Martin Luther King's "I Have a Dream" speech, or Neil Armstrong's first words on the moon. Dentists have conventions. Actors have their award ceremonies. Musicians and fans their concerts, anthropologists and sociologists their annual meetings, athletes their games. These excessively public, excessively social events often hold in suspended animation the difficulties our too human conceits create between black and white, rich and poor, male and female. Dense, exciting, during these assemblies the usual rules governing social interaction slip back behind the electricity of the catch, the game, the event.

Yet they never last. At the end of herring season, all through the previous three centuries, the women put away their knives and the men hung up the nets for storage. The woodsmen trickled back into the pines, and the fugitive slaves, carrying wages, whiskey, and fish, slipped back into the swamp.

Around the time the herring season was ending, another fishery was just getting under way, this one less momentous in character, consisting of families who spotted and chased whales and porpoises along the Outer Banks. These early whalers may have helped haul the seines during March, but the whale migrations began in the spring and the peak season fell during the months of April and May. The annual marine mammal movements inspired two types of whaling: pelagic whaling, or that done by big ships following herds across the Atlantic, similar to the whaling portrayed on Herman Melville's Pequod; and coastal, shore-based whaling, where a small boat or group of boats would pursue whales and porpoises over a much smaller geographical range. All the pelagic whaling done in North Carolina waters was done by ships whose home ports were outside the state, mostly in New England. North Carolina's home-grown whaling industry never grew from a shore enterprise into a pelagic enterprise.

Early whaling in the Mid-Atlantic, whether conducted from shore or from the big New England ships, entangled whalers and politicians in what must have been the earliest commercial fishing-licensing issues along the Atlantic Coast. Whale oil and bone were among the dearest commodities of the day, the oil used as a lubricant and fuel—for lighting, ease of movement, and warmth—and the bone used in products requiring toughness and flexibility, such as buggy whips, shirt collars, hoops in women's skirts, and corset stays. In their pamphlet on whaling in North Carolina, Marcus and Sallie Simpson tell us that whale oil was used as currency, appearing in court records of debt settlements, tax payments, and fine payments. As a valued commodity, whales emerged early in disputes over rights to North Carolina's coastal resources. These disputes occurred among coastal residents and landowners as well as between government authority and private citizens.

Disputes over the disposition of whales and whale products derived, in part, from the ways coastal dwellers and visitors encountered them. Some of the earliest disputes on record involved whales that had drifted ashore, helpless, disoriented, their directional apparatus malfunctioning. Whales in such a state make easy prey, and anyone finding one in Colonial Virginia or North Carolina must have felt as if they had stumbled across a chest of gold. But finding a beached whale was more like finding a wallet full of money with the owner's identification wedged between the bills, impossible to miss, for all whales belonged to the crown and its representatives—the governors and proprietors—and access to whales depended on either obtaining a license to whale or whaling beyond the reach of the court's authority. Early coastal settlers engaged in both strategies, with those who merely possessed licenses often bringing charges against those who laid claim to beached whales through hard work.

That disputes of this nature took place tells something about the people inhabiting Mid-Atlantic barrier islands during the Colonial period. On the one hand there were those who acquired licenses, followed the ways of authority, and stood to benefit from the status quo; on the other hand there were those who circumvented government authority, claiming beached whales through days and days of hard work, involving their entire families in cutting and trying out oil and bleaching bone.

Ironically, the courts did not uniformly support the claims of those licensed to whale over families who invested their time and sweat in whale processing. A court decision involving a licensee named Mathais Towler and a family headed by Anne Ros forced Towler to pay Ros for the effort her family had expended rendering oil from a beached whale. We do not know whether the Ros family would have done better to have sold the whale products themselves, but they probably would have. North Carolina historian David Stick tells us that crews lucky enough to land whales from Diamond City, in the mid-nineteenth century, could expect as much as $4,000 per animal, and in her local history of Salter Path, Kay Stephens tells a story about how the mere expectation of earnings from whaling prompted wives to smoke their entire household store of tobacco.

Whaling occupied an ambiguous position in early North Carolina's political and economic landscape. Unlike the plantation-based herring fisheries, landing and processing whales required only a few household and community members working cooperatively. To process drift whales, families and community members pooled their labor quickly, dividing up the work as efficiently as they could before the whale's flesh deteriorated. Reading about these whale-processing gatherings reminds me of similar passages describing the BaMbuti Pygmies of Central Africa, who move their entire camp to the carcass of a fallen elephant, feasting on the great beast's meat. People along North Carolina's coast established temporary residence around dead whales, setting up lean-tos and shelters and taking their meals near the carcass until they finished taking the oil, meat, and bone. Together, working at high speed, they cut away huge slabs of skin and blubber, set up iron kettles over fires near the carcass, boiled the flesh and skimmed off the oil, and wrested the bones from the body and head. David Stick, writing about Diamond City, describes a practice that may have been inspired by the biblical story of Jonah: "Uncle Billy Hancock's job was to cut out the bone in the whale's mouth. He wore a suit of oilskins, fitted tight so there was hardly a piece of him that wasn't covered; then he'd take his ax and go in the whale's mouth. Sometimes he'd disappear inside, and you could hear him cutting away with his ax; then he'd come out again, bringing a piece of mouth bone with him."

Early coastal dwellers acquired their taste for oil, meat, and bone from processing drift whales, but it did not take them long to engage the big mammals in their own element, usually preying on mother Right Whales after cornering their young. As early as the seventeenth century, they spotted and then chased live whales, capturing them with such high-seas drama that they felt compelled to name each victim. What began as the opportunistic processing of beached whales evolved, during the eighteenth and nineteenth centuries, into a small fishery of seasonal whaling camps operating all along the barrier islands. The best-known and most highly organized camps were established on Shackleford Banks, where about eighteen men took turns manning lookout shelters for passing whales. Along other sections of the coast, the whaling crews were less specialized and more intertwined with the daily activities of the coast; between whale sightings families tended gardens and livestock, fished, combed beaches for firewood. But whether highly organized or not, a whale sighting electrified groups of men and boys into action, typically involving an extended pursuit by several swift rowboats, a capture and kill, and then the long process of landing and processing the whale.

Probably the most notable characteristic of these shore-based whalers was their tendency to name their victims, a practice restricted to North Carolina. Whales were named after their captors (Lee Whale, Tom Martin Whale), for the weather (Cold Sunday, a day so cold, it was said, waterfowl froze in flight), or for unique circumstances surrounding their capture. One named Little Children Whale was so named because mostly young men participated in its capture. Another was named after George Washington, landed on his birthday, and yet another, Mayflower, whose bones today hang in the Carolina Museum of Natural History in Raleigh, drug its captors seven miles out to sea before succumbing to repeated harpoon attacks. They were able to name each whale because they caught only a few every spring and each landing had something

Whaler Josephus Willis Sr., Carteret County, North Carolina, c. 1884

memorable about it, something unique. Whether the name honored the whale or the whaler depended on the particular character of the chase, the engagement, and the kill.

But the name was not as important as the fact that they were named, demonstrating that each episode of whaling was memorable. Today the descendants of these whalers, scattered around neighborhoods in Beaufort and Morehead City, still lay claim to this heritage in their family histories, calling themselves Ca'e Bankers and finding unity and identity in their Tidewater English, their Scottish and English surnames, their traditions of hunting and eating loons, and their enduring relationship to the sea. That their ancestral Ca'e Bankers could recount whaling episodes reflected the nature of their interaction with these great seagoing mammals and, by extension, with the sea itself.

Remember that they never made the transition from shore to pelagic whaling. At the season's end, they moved on to mullet fishing and clamming, gigging flounder, crabbing, and raising livestock and farming. In short, they never became industrialized fishers, never sailed vessels where the crew, whales, and even the captains became interchangeable, roaming the high seas. They might migrate up and down the coast for brief seasonal fishing excursions, or set up temporary shelters and blinds to hunt waterfowl on remote strands of barrier islands, but these early North Carolina whalers never strayed too far for too long from the families and communities of coastal North Carolina. Their histories, their identities, were local, unique, spawning the distinctive Tidewater English dialects reminiscent of Elizabethan England and the carving and boatbuilding traditions that persist today in the seasonal contours of their lives.

The same cannot be said of the planter-fishers who organized the herring fisheries from the heart and soul of the British Empire and the antebellum South. Far from building identities from local traditions and materials, they were export and import oriented, drawing cultural cues from distant aristocracies and courtly manners forged in estate houses and the pages of Jane Austen's novels. After the Civil War, this external outlook turned back on them and, ironically, the harvest of herring fell to the control of ordinary people.

Two Union soldiers who witnessed the herring fishery during the war returned in the middle 1860s to introduce a fishing gear they learned to use in the fisheries of the Great Lakes, the pound net—or, as it was called then, the pod net or Dutch net, because the Union soldiers came from Pennsylvania. This simple diffusion of innovation revolutionized the fishery, undermining the dominance of the plantations in the herring harvest and stimulating a lengthy series of court disputes. These disputes pitted the small family fisher against an industrialized fishery that, during its height in the mid-nineteenth century, organized 28 haul seine-based fisheries, employed more than 5,000 Carolinians, and operated 200 vessels.

Compared with the haul seine, which required these great mobilizing operations and continuous infusions of capital, pound nets required the labor of but one or two men and involved far less cash. The net itself—actually an apparatus of several nets—is curiously shaped, consisting of a set of usually three pound nets, or empoundments, connected to a long, fence-like net that extends out into the river or sound, perpendicular to the shore. It is based on the ancient principle of the fish weir, one of the oldest fishing techniques in the world, which channels fish into an enclosure by means of a set of poles or stakes. John White's drawings of the Algonquin peoples depict shallow-water fish weirs in the backgrounds of fishing scenes. Both weirs and pound nets are designed to channel and entrap fish. Two chambers of the pound net are heart- or arrow-shaped, and the third, the principal enclosure from which fish are dipped, is either rectangular or square and fitted with a funnel coming in from the nearest chamber. All the chambers and the long, fence-like nets are fastened to the bottom by means of long stakes that protrude a foot or so above water. The entire apparatus seems to point to the last rectangular empoundment, which can fill with as many as 10,000 pounds of fish a day.

The productivity of the pound net, and the fact that one or two men could construct and fish with it, were qualities that were not welcomed

Men checking a pound net, Colerain, North Carolina, c. 1939

by the big haul-seine fisheries. Until the Civil War, the herring fishery was dominated by the haul-seine operations described earlier, which organized both the harvesting and the processing of the fish. The war interrupted these activities and dealt a crippling blow to the big haul-seiner for three reasons. First, of course, the heavy reliance on plantation slave labor suffered under increasing opportunities for slaves to escape during the chaos of war or to be liberated by Union troops. Second, confederate politicians outlawed herring fishing in 1863, fearing that the high-quality proteins produced by the fishery would, through various black markets or outright confiscation, fuel Union armies against the Confederacy. And third, it was the Union occupation of eastern North Carolina that exposed two fishers from Pennsylvania to the herring fishery, leading them to introduce pound nets first into the Croatan Sound and later into Albemarle and the big rivers emptying into the estuary.

The haul-seiners, back in business in a reduced capacity after the war, did not readily relinquish their hold over the herring stocks. It took twenty-five years of court battles, twenty-five years of engaging and revising first ideas and then legal definitions and finally laws about commons and private property. The pound net initially squeezed into waters between the big fisheries along Albemarle, stimulating lawsuits such as those involving the Hettrick brothers, which came before North Carolina's Supreme Court first in 1875 and again in 1880.

In 1873, the Hettricks purchased acreage known as the Snow Hill Place, on the north shore of Albemarle, just west of the Long Beach Fishery, a herring fishery owned and operated by C. W. Skinner with haul seines. That February, just before the arrival of the first herring and shad of the season, the Hettricks drove several long stakes out into Albemarle's soft bottom, extending a mile into the sound, perpendicular to their property, and strung a pound net out into the water. Skinner appealed to the Hettricks to place their stakes farther west, where they would not interfere with the working and drifting of his haul seine. On windy days, Skinner claimed, the haul seine could drift as much as a quarter of a mile upstream or down, where it might become entangled in the Hettrick brothers' stakes.

If Skinner's first visits to the Hettricks were friendly and then beseeching, offering to help the brothers move the stakes farther west, Skinner later involved the courts and the sheriff to remove the Hettricks' stakes. By the time the case reached the state supreme court in 1875, the state legislature had passed a law making it illegal to place a pound net within a half-mile of the outside windlasses that operated a fishery's haul seine. The court ruled that the Hettricks' stakes unjustly interfered with Skinner's haul seine, crippling a business that, the judges said, cost between $15,000 and $20,000 a year to operate and generated "receipts generally from $20,000 to $30,000 annually, at that and other similar fisheries on the sound." The Hettricks' investment, by contrast, was a mere $5,000.

Thus the court's ruling, along with the 1874–75 law passed by the legislature, supported the haul-seine fishery against the pound nets, justi-

Woman with shotgun ferrying deer on the New River, North Carolina, c. 1895

fying their decisions by citing the economic importance of the larger operations. Such economic arguments wind through the entire history of conflicts over the allocation of fisheries and the rights of those who own property along the coast, emerging even today in disputes between commercial and recreational fishers and between old and new residents in coastal villages. Again in 1880 and 1888, cases brought before the state supreme court ended in judgments against the pound nets and in favor of the haul-seine fisheries.

Yet legal backing was not enough to stop trends in the coastal economy. Haul-seiners found it ever more difficult to recruit workers to the hauling of their nets. By the first decade of the twentieth century, only a handful of haul-seine fisheries remained; by mid-century, most haul-seine fisheries had either gone out of business or become specialized herring salting and packing facilities, leaving the harvesting of herring up to the pound-netters and, later, gill-netters who operated independently of the centralized and highly capitalized fisheries. The pound and gill nets were too efficient, less dependent on large numbers of workers who became more and more difficult to recruit or coerce into fishing after first the Civil War and then World Wars I and II. Eventually, the big haul-seiners pulled back, stowed their gear ashore, and settled into processing and marketing the catch, leaving the water, the harvest of herring, to the many small fishers manning gill and pound nets along the shore.

VANISHING WOMEN

When haul-seiners withdrew from the herring harvest, they did not go far. The labor advantages of pound-netting and gill-netting may have pushed them off the water, but the cutting, salting, packing, and shipping of herring still required a level of organization and investment that was beyond the means of most independent netters. So when they withdrew, they withdrew only as far as the fish-processing facilities along the shore. They no longer set their seines from their own boats, yet the owners of the big herring-processing plants still remained the primary organizational force of the herring fishery, the linchpins that held together the harvesting, processing, and marketing sectors.

The same pattern is found today in the herring and shad fisheries and in most other fisheries in the state. From creaking complexes of docks, weighing scales, cleaning and picking tables, conveyor belts, and parking lots paved with decades of shell and bone, seafood processors buy fish and shellfish from fishers, run them through the hands of thousands of coastal workers, and truck them, usually to Baltimore and New York, to sell. At the core of these operations are workers—women and men who take seasonal, low-paying, generally unpleasant jobs shucking scallops and oysters, cutting fish, grading clams, and picking the sweet white meat from blue crabs. The herring fisheries may be the state's most mammoth fishing operations, hiring the most workers at the cutting and salting plants, but they operate for only a few weeks a year and in a narrow region of the state.

In the saltwater and brackish waterways of the Mid-Atlantic Coast, however, the seafood industry most hungry for hired hands is the one based on the cantankerous blue crab. Every spring, these wily crustaceans climb out of winter retreats of mud, moving into the creeks, rivers, sounds, and bays, making slow and treacherous passage from the inland corridors of water and wetlands toward the open sea. The passage is treacherous because they must tiptoe past thousands of traps, resisting the temptations of ripe fish in the bait holds, ducking the rakes of crab scrapers, or letting go of trot lines baited with chicken necks before the line's owner dips his net. Between the northern reaches of the Chesapeake Bay and Cape Fear, this dance of predator and prey can last as long as ten months, from February to November. The peak season is the summer, when salinity levels shift in ways that signal the crabs to move. From late May to September, from east of North Carolina's Currituck Sound to the westernmost ripples of the Pamlico River, along the James, York, Rappahannock Rivers in Virginia and all around the Chesapeake Bay, crab-picking plants come alive with boats, trucks, workers, and fresh blue crabs.

Picking the sweet white meat from blue crabs demands patience and a level of technical skill appreciated by anyone who has ever performed the task. It isn't easy work. One reason the lovely white lump meat, free of shell, sometimes commands more than $14.00 a pound is that most people would rather have women in remote concrete buildings pick the meat from the crabs than tear up their own fingers. The legendary orneriness of the crab lasts even after death. Pincers aside, dead crabs, cooked to a beautiful orange and cooled, continue sticking, scratching, and slicing human skin from sentries of twenty sharp shell points along their armor's edge.

Women receive them at work stations in shovelfuls—literally. Men use shovels to keep piles of the cooked crustaceans in front of the women. Then the women take them up one after another and work a knife under and then around the rim of each carapace, lifting off the top and separating viscera and fat from meat with further deft swipes of the knife. The women who perform this task, in most picking houses, earn piece rates instead of hourly wages. The big "lump" crabmeat pays $1.70 to $2.00 a pound, while the flakes and shavings from the legs and more inaccessible reaches of the crab's insides may bring only $1.35 or $1.50 a pound, and the fat and refuse, used for pet foods, as little as 50 cents. On a good day a good picker can earn up to $60 or $70, but most earn around $40. Frustrating earning capability is the supply of crab, rising and falling daily and weekly through the season. On some days the vanishing women have gone through all the cooked crab by 10 o'clock in the morning, picking only a few pounds apiece. On other days, the vanishing women arrive at first light and stay well into the afternoon.

Why vanishing? Because, historically, North Carolina's crab pickers slipped into the recesses of coastal counties after leaving the plants. Daily and at the end of the season, they returned to neighborhoods along back roads and inside small coastal communities that few people who eat the fruits of their labor ever see. These are vibrant, industrious neighborhoods where people express their creativity in the living strategies of just getting by, mining opportunity from the tiniest of deposits in the coastal economy and society. Typically, in these settings, household members pool their energies and needs into common family accounts. Whenever I visit one of these family complexes—or complex families—I am struck by the variety and character of the ways in which they reach into the land, water, industry, and society of the coast to make ends meet. Summers, during the height of the crab-picking season, I enjoy visiting these neighborhoods and writing in my field journals passages telling about the ways the surface appearances of houses and yards re-

Woman picking crab, Aurora, North Carolina, c. 1990

flect the human ingenuity beneath. A pen of hunting hounds reveals a family's reliance on wild game. Gill nets dry between pines, only one of several physical manifestations of a household's deep and intimate attachments to the estuary. In the inventory of rummage sales, you can read vignettes about local skills, local opportunities, local crafts: hand-carved swan and duck decoys, equipment for clearing land and watering livestock, overhauled outboard motors, cider presses, home-whittled hooks for hanging hams to smoke on long Sunday afternoons. . . . In a passage I wrote some years ago, I characterized the countryside around the crab plants like this:

> These are, at times, depressing areas. Yet some people demonstrate a belligerent independence, reflected in the wide range of small-scale, independent, domestically based businesses throughout the countryside. In addition to low-wage and seasonal work, they sell whatever they can produce with limited means: honey, duck de-

coys, farm produce, seafood, ceramic figurines, lawn furniture. Services they provide include hairdressing and cosmetology; they are craftsmen, repair people, upholsterers, notaries, palm readers and advisors, and people who prepare income taxes or stuff and lick envelopes at home for some mail marketing firm. Into society such as this, defense contractors subcontract the wrapping of semiconductors with wire and other detailed and monotonous tasks that don't need security clearances. It is not uncommon to see the equipment of two or three small enterprises littering someone's yard—say, crab pots, a tractor, and a carpenter's pickup truck. Combined with these may be gardens, livestock pens, antlers, cut wood, and fish skeletons, all indicating heavy reliance on the land for food, shelter, and fuel.

Until the late 1980s, the owners of crab-processing plants hired women from neighborhoods like these because the mix of economic resources allowed crab pickers to rotate among several trades, coming and going from the crab-picking plants as supplies of crabs rose and fell. Salinity levels, fertility, fish kills, state regulations, the shifting of crabbers' loyalties from one plant to another—all these and dozens of other unpredictable factors can influence the number of crabs any one plant has for the picking. Crab-picking plants need workers who can move with the ebb and flow of the crabs—that is, workers who have several sources of income and other productive activities to keep them attached to their neighborhoods, who are capable of supporting themselves when there is no work in the plants, yet dependent enough on income from crab picking that they remain available for work when crabs arrive at the plants. It is a delicate balance the owners of crab houses must achieve, encouraging their workers to be dependent yet independent, tied to the plants yet also capable of withdrawing into creative consumption and production strategies when work in the plants slows. The price plant owners have paid for this balance, over the years, has been worker reliability.

Flora Willis's circumstance is typical. She works for a small crab picker in Belhaven, near the confluence of the Pungo and Pamlico Rivers, using income from crab picking to cover the bulk of her household's expenses during the summer months. During the off-season, she cleans houses for three elderly women while signing up for unemployment compensation and withdrawing into her networks of friends and kin. Her husband works for a forestry company, and one of her sons strings a trot line for brim in the irrigation canals crisscrossing Hyde County. She donates time to the church and cares for the children of friends called away to tend to their sick, bury their dead, or visit their incarcerated, accumulating favors that may or may not come back as gifts of friendship, things, or time.

Flora's several responsibilities at home and in the African-American community mean that, at times, when Will Irons, the handyman at the crab plant, sends a van into Flora's neighborhood to take crab pickers to the plant, Flora must decline the invitation. Gordy Striker, a processing-plant owner in Beaufort County, once looked at me severely when I asked him how many pickers he expected to have working the following day. Something in his look pitied my stupidity. He softened and said, "Son, you never know. There might be twenty pickers standing at the front door when I open in the morning. There might be two. You just never know."

This is the worker reliability problem I just mentioned, the unpredictability of workers who have alternate sources of income, from small gardens and casual beauty salons to state and federal assistance programs. Traditionally, plant owners like Striker attacked the problem of worker reliability by subtly infiltrating the homes and neighborhoods of women who worked at their plants. This infiltration was not a clandestine or even a particularly underhanded process. It was, as I said, subtle, based on the simple practice of using women who currently worked in the plants to recruit new workers. During the 1980s, whenever I visited plants, it was not at all uncommon to find several African-American women and young girls related to one another through what anthropologists call uterine ties—kin relations, that is, established through mothers. Simply, older women brought their daughters and granddaughters to the crab plants to work beside or across from them at the picking tables, maternal aunts brought nieces, cousins related through mothers and sisters brought each other.

This practice solved two dimensions of the worker reliability problem. Most obvious, of course, is that workers became available to work as soon as they reached an age where they could pick crab. In some plants I met girls as young as thirteen years old picking crab, although more commonly they began at age fifteen or sixteen. A second benefit of recruiting through kinship was that plant owners tapped into the authority that elder women exercise over their granddaughters and daughters, nieces, and younger siblings and cousins. They drew that household, family-based authority into the plants, relying on the elder women to discipline their younger relatives for not showing up for work or for misbehaving at the picking tables.

The system was not perfect. Workers' loyalties, ultimately, lay with their kin, and they were willing to exercise authority over the youth, on behalf of plant owners, only as long as crab picking was at the core of all their household economic activities. This worked for four generations. In counties like Pamlico, you could fish, hunt, raise a few goats, or plant or cut trees for Weyerhaeuser, but the county's industrial base did not provide a wide range of steady year-round jobs. Alternatives to picking crab were rare, and within the unwritten human calculus that guides the ways people select jobs, there was the knowledge that crab picking at least allowed some flexibility of scheduling as the crab supplies fluctuated. A family could tend to its domestic schedules, which were also flexible, and still supply workers for the plants.

Some time during the early 1980s, the balance of power began to shift. The authority the crab-plant owners wielded over their workers, ultimately enforced through elder black women, lost some of its punch. Slowly, even glacially, the gains of the civil rights movement reached into the recesses of Pamlico, Beaufort, and other rural coastal counties, and the ice pack of an undifferentiated economy began breaking up. A few new opportunities opened up for African-American women, and some of the old stand-bys expanded. Between 1980 and 1990, the labor force of the big crab-picking county of Pamlico grew by 27 percent and Beaufort by 17 percent, reflecting jobs and interest in these areas generated by tourism, seasonal and retirement living, and the increases in health care associated with caring for the elderly.

Combined, these developments allowed, even encouraged, African-American women to resist the local authority of crab-plant owners. Few behaviors are more inspiring than acts of resistance among oppressed, downtrodden peoples. After ten years of working in low-wage, dead-end jobs and nearly twenty years of anthropological fieldwork, I have had the good luck to see people ranging from Iowa waterworks technicians to Minnesota carpenters, from Jamaican peasants and sugarcane cutters to Puerto Rican fishers, and from Haitian chicken workers to Mayan farmworkers swim against the tides of authority. I have seen them use subtle, often amusing methods that feed on pretense and deception to accomplish their goals of frustrating pushy foremen, bossy bosses, condescending supervisors, cruel labor contractors, and paternalistic owners of crab-picking plants. The African-American women of coastal North Carolina can resist with the best of them. It is lovely to watch a small, quiet women, a woman of seventy with a depth of experience, deflect a request of her boss to bring her granddaughters to work. She smiles, shyly and sweetly, as if he might be asking her to a school dance, but she refuses to give a direct answer and says only, "Why, Mr. Striker, the children these days don't hardly seem like they want to work."

At home they were telling a different story. At home they were encouraging their daughters and their daughters' daughters and nieces to take courses at the community college. They were telling them to fill their summer months with more regular paychecks, working in the expanding tourist industry or even, if need be, leaving the county for better job prospects in Havelock, Morehead City, Greenville, and New Bern. They were saying, "Do anything, anything at all, to prevent a lifetime of picking crab."

In this way the umbilical cord of authority, the link between production and reproduction that ran between crab plants and black neighborhoods, broke. Plant owners lost their control over the reproduction of the labor force, lost their ability to infiltrate households effectively. The balance, the subtle give-and-take between flexible schedules and worker reliability, was gone. By the mid-1980s, the labor crisis had become critical. Blue-crab meat production began to fall and plants began to close. In Belhaven, one of the oldest seafood plants in North Carolina closed—his neighbor told me—"for lack of pickers." Something, it was clear, had to be done.

Mary McGuire knew the crab-picking business as well as anyone. Her family's three plants on the western shores of the Chesapeake had been founded by her father. By the late 1980s, her father had phased back his participation in the family business, and Mary assumed the helm, smoothly and expertly entering the business, like most daughters and wives, from the ground floor. Mary stood beside the women at the crab-picking tables more than a few times over the years. She had sold crab and fish from the family's seafood market, cooked in their restaurant, waited tables, carried dishes, steamed crabs. She had seen to the books, met with crabbers and buyers, organized shipments, and seen to every aspect of plant maintenance at every one of the family's plants.

Mary was a small, pretty woman, well-spoken, with straight blonde hair and a stylish practicality about her dress that suggested she could negotiate a bank loan down by three percentage points as easily as sit in the plant lunchroom with her pickers. The day I first met her she was both warm and precise, careful without being guarded, confident that her reading of the recent change in her labor force was accurate. She quoted production statistics and personal anecdotes to verify everything she told me. But she did not need to convince me. I'd heard variations on her story again and again throughout tidewater Virginia and North Carolina and along the western edge of Maryland's lower eastern shore. Pickers were leaving the plants without bothering to refer new workers. Their networks were tapped out. Ads in newspapers and other more conventional recruiting techniques, rarely used in the past, brought

Mary fifty new workers to the plants, forty-nine of whom quit after the training period.

Yet Mary McGuire was a kind of pioneer, moving into a frontier of new labor reserves without fully comprehending what she was getting into. It's like that with pioneers. They move forward cautiously, without the benefit of accurate intelligence or a full view of what lies ahead. Most of today's trailblazers, of course, aren't moving into unknown mountain chains or rain forests, but forever expanding into the shifting landscapes of culture and society, drawing new ethnic identities and cultural practices into the body of knowledge, mapping local histories, digging new political and economic canals over which flow new workers, new systems of credit, new ways of organizing old places of work.

Faced with labor supply problems in industries like seafood processing, employers like Mary McGuire usually go first to their employees for referrals, second to conventional private channels such as newspaper ads, and finally, often as a last resort, to the public sector—those state and local offices that attempt to link unemployed workers with job openings. These are the same offices, usually, where people who are out of work sign up for unemployment compensation and periodically turn in reports about what they have been doing to get off the dole. When I first met Ralph Wallace, the man working for the Virginia Employment Security Commission whom Mary McGuire visited when her labor force began dwindling, he joked, "This isn't the employment office, don't you know? It's the *un*employment office."

To be quite honest, after more than fifteen years of working on labor market problems in the United States, I'm still in the dark about the exact relationships between state employment security commissions, Departments of Labor, Occupational Health and Safety Administrations, and the myriad of employment and unemployment compensation services each of these provides. They are mazes of bureaucracies within bureaucracies, with wires for funds running from Washington, D.C., to state capitals across the country. Inside them, over the years, I have run across individuals who cared so deeply about workers' rights that they were willing to join strikers on picket lines and those so adamant about the industry's need for cheap labor that they proposed programs to import workers from other countries whenever local workers began to loaf.

Ralph Wallace advocated importing workers. In fact, he had devoted a good portion of his career to exactly the business of helping apple growers bring in workers from Jamaica for the harvests. When I first met him, in the late 1980s, he was nearing retirement and looking around for additional work to supplement his pension. He was a short man, with closely cropped hair and spectacles, and somewhat guarded and cagey in his responses to my questions. At that time I was studying the apple industry that stretches from Roanoke to Hendersonville along the Blue Ridge Mountains, taking a break from interviewing farmers and farmworkers to see what people in Richmond had to say about America's most patriotic fruit.

Have you ever visited a state agency with a vague or quirky inquiry? What commonly happens is that you get shuffled from receptionist to receptionist, from office to office, and from floor to floor, until these referrals begin to snowball and coalesce and you find yourself in a remote cubicle of a remote department facing someone who comes across as remote.

Ralph Wallace looked at me suspiciously the first time we met, but he warmed up quickly when he heard that I was putting together a research project for the U.S. Department of Labor. Gradually it became clear that he wanted me to involve him in my research as a paid consultant. We spoke several times over the next few months, each time meeting with more and more people at the Virginia Employment Commission, leading up to a meeting with U.S. Department of Labor personnel to discuss transferring large sums of money from Washington to Richmond. As these meetings drew more and more people out of their offices and cubicles, I was able to observe Ralph within the network of his co-workers. They relied on him, I saw, for certain information related to specific employers. He was widely respected as one of the main people in the office familiar with Virginia's labor force dynamics at the ground level. He joked about himself, deprecating himself in front of his co-

workers in an easy, country lawyer way, pretending to know less than
he knew. I recall one meeting where he said, "I'm just a crazy old man
getting ready for retirement."

At this his boss turned to me and said, "Crazy like a fox."

It was Ralph Wallace who helped Mary McGuire bring in women
from Mexico to pick her crabs. He had a whole career of experience
behind him. Since World War II, Virginia apple growers had been using
a little-known program administered by the U.S. Department of Labor
that allowed them to bring in Jamaicans to harvest their fruit. Several
features of the program were highly controversial, challenged in courts
of law many times over the years. Once during the late 1970s, the Department of Labor even brought in Puerto Ricans—who are citizens,
after all—to replace the Jamaicans, but the apple growers marshaled
community and state support against them. A judge and Senator Byrd
stepped in and forced the Puerto Ricans to go back home.

Why would apple growers insist on having Jamaican pickers when
there were Puerto Rican pickers on hand to pick their fruit? It gets
back to questions of worker reliability and workplace discipline. The
Jamaicans are authorized to work for a single employer. They are
housed, fed, doctored, and shuttled from orchard to orchard by their
employers. Because Puerto Ricans are U.S. citizens, they have all kinds
of rights that protect them against abusive employers. If the growers
treat them badly, they have the option to leave, just as the vanishing
women of the crab plants had the options to shrink back into their
families, their crafts, and their gardens when the owners of crab plants
yelled at them too loudly or placed too many demands on their pace of
work.

Now Mary McGuire, with Ralph Wallace's help, had found what
seemed to be the answer to that delicate imbalance of power: temporary,
foreign, seasonal women. These would be women who were used to
making $5 a day, used to living in homes without indoor plumbing,
used to relying on public transportation to get around. These would be
women, Mary McGuire and Ralph Wallace believed, who would be
happy to come to the United States to spend eight months picking white

meat from blue crabs and living in dormitories without their families, with little freedom and unable to wash the smell of crab from their skin.

I spoke about the transition from African-American to Mexican labor in the blue-crab industry as part of a lecture series at the Duke University Marine Laboratory in Beaufort, North Carolina, in the fall of 1994. Since pioneers like Mary McGuire and Ralph Wallace arranged to bring in some of the first foreign workers, Mexican women had been coming into the blue-crab processing plants at an ever growing pace. By the 1993 season, several complaints from these women accumulated against some owners of crab plants. In July 1993, after stories of abuses of the Mexican women appeared in the *Wall Street Journal* and several state and local newspapers, the U.S. Department of Labor commissioned me and two of my colleagues—Monica Heppel and Luis Torres of the Inter-American Institute on Migration and Labor—to look into the labor practices in several industries that, like the blue-crab industry, import women with the aid of special visas. By the time of my talk at Duke, we had interviewed more than 400 workers and just under 100 employers using temporary alien labor, including the women and bosses in the crab houses, Jamaican chambermaids in Myrtle Beach, and Mexican men manning shrimp vessels in Texas, working in horseracing stables in Arizona and California, and quarrying ornamental stone in Idaho.

The audience at the Duke laboratory, however, was interested only in the workers coming into the crab plants. I gave them all the numbers—piece rates, hours worked per day and week, pounds of crab—and described the dormitories and relationships between workers and employers and other aspects of the job, then explained how employers preferred Mexican workers over African-American workers because the Mexicans were easier to control. They were, quite simply, more reliable, their behaviors more predictable, because plant owners housed them at or close to the plants and assumed responsibility for transporting them and generally moving them from community to community in eastern North Carolina, Virginia, and Maryland, thus avoiding the labor-reliability problems that plagued relying on African-American workers.

After I finished my talk, a young economist in the audience began pestering me with irrelevant questions. She wanted to know, for example, how much crab-plant owners were paying for fresh crabs. Prices varied over the season, I said. She kept pressing for information about expenses. How much for utilities, taxes, equipment? Finally I asked her why she wanted to know. Obviously already indoctrinated into the ideology of rational cost accounting, she said, "I should think you would want to know about operating expenses before studying labor."

I smiled. I realized that she hadn't followed my argument: the crab processors' decision to use Mexicans, and their behaviors toward the women, were based not merely on operating expenses but primarily on labor control.

This was not the first time I had encountered an economist who had trouble thinking outside of the narrow confines of cost accounting. While some of the best social science comes from economists who consider social and cultural contexts important—who, in short, communicate with sociologists and anthropologists—many economic studies draw conclusions more from assumptions than from facts. Economic science rests on certain theoretical principles and methods of analysis that encourage some of its practitioners to reduce human behavior to dollars and cents. But reducing the transition to Mexican labor to the forces of the marketplace is as misleading as considering the Alligator River National Wildlife Refuge just another piece of land. Bringing Mexican women into the crab plants involved, in fact, direct political manipulation of the market for labor, making an analysis based on marketplace factors irrelevant at best and, at worst, misleading. Crab-plant owners like Mary McGuire and former bureaucrats like Ralph Wallace, together with all kinds of state and federal Department of Labor personnel, manipulated the market much as wildlife biologists tinker with the populations of hybrid striped bass in hatcheries, or animal scientists manipulate the reproductive habits of chickens and hogs.

My talk drew these very parallels. The growing use of Mexican women in the crab industry is similar to relationships of hostility and symbiosis we find in nature. Some of this may have come through in the

Mexican and black women picking crab, Aurora, North Carolina, c. 1990

previous discussion on the vanishing women, how they slipped in and out of crab-picking plants according to the schedules of home enterprises as much as to time clocks. Their relationships with plant owners combined elements of symbiosis as well as predator and prey.

We find a similar relationship between groupers and wrasses around ocean reefs. Usually, these two fish—the big, ungainly grouper and the sleek and tiny wrass—help one another deal with shifting food supplies and gentle accumulations of crud on fish scales. Under normal conditions, the wrass cleans the grouper's scales by eating the gradual build-ups of algae and other organic matter. Normally, the two get along well, the one providing a service, the other a food. Yet from time to time their relationship falters. The wrass, in its haste to keep the grouper clean, sometimes takes a piece of the grouper, biting off a mouthful of flesh. Nor is the grouper always a passive, benevolent host, for on occasion, feeling lazy perhaps, and hungry, the grouper eats the wrass.

Such symbiotic, delicately imbalanced relationships occur in human societies all the time. Workers pilfering from employers, or employers crippling workers, are examples of symbiotic relationships gone awry. Around an ocean reef, eventually, these imbalances work themselves out through genetics and selective pressures in populations, where the wilier of the wrasses manage to elude capture, and the more tolerant of the grouper keep clean of crud. By contrast, humans are often far too impatient to wait for generations to pass and for imbalances to correct themselves. We restock rivers and lakes with trout and bass and reintroduce wild animals into wild habitats after generations of breeding in zoos.

Mid-Atlantic coastal residents are no strangers to these practices. Since the 1970s, fisheries biologists have been tinkering with the population dynamics of hybrid striped bass, creating barriers to catching the fish that have been so effective that now striped bass clog gill nets and hinder effective commercial fishing. In 1987, the Alligator River National Wildlife Refuge garnered the nation's attention when wildlife conservationists released rare red wolves into the pine and cypress trees. And in 1989, in a handful of crab plants in North Carolina, Virginia, and Maryland, public and private interests joined to supplement the blue crab picking labor force, bringing in young Mexican women as though dropping hatchlings from an airplane into an ancient lake.

Whenever humans interfere with natural reproductive cycles, their surrounding environments respond in unpredictable and unforeseen ways. Carp in midwestern rivers, starlings throughout the United States, rabbits in Australia, and zebra mussels choking the intake valves of power plants near the Great Lakes are all examples of organisms introduced into foreign natural settings where, without natural predators, they bred like crazy and quickly became nuisances. Immigration regulations in the United States are similar to biologists' attempts to supplement natural reproductive processes. When there are too few jobs in the country to go around, the government moves to restrict immigration, tightening visa requirements, lowering quotas, beefing up border patrols, and the like. When labor scarcities develop, the government relaxes restrictions and lets more immigrants in, sometimes even promoting immigration with the aid of state programs and new kinds of visas.

Rarely do changing immigration policies influence only the labor force. In Germany during the 1980s, witnessing the rising tide of white supremacy directed toward Turks and Pakistanis who came into the country as guest workers following World War II, the German labor minister said, "We thought we were importing workers, but we were importing people." In Virginia, Maryland, and North Carolina, the owners of crab plants bringing in women from Mexico also thought they were importing only workers. At first, many of the plant owners treated them as if they were only workers, confining them in small areas in small towns, and in some cases keeping them fenced in, virtually imprisoned. As though suffering from pent-up demand, some processors worked these women day in, day out, buying more crab than they ever had, opening new lines, introducing new products. In the first three years of the program, crabmeat production in North Carolina rose from 8.9 million to 10.8 million pounds. Their competitors in Maryland and Virginia claimed to be using the Mexican women merely to keep production stable, complaining that North Carolina processors used the program to expand, holding the Mexican women's noses to the grindstone of picking, picking, picking ever more crab. And it was true: some North Carolina processors had them working before dawn and on nights and weekends. Gradually, the Mexican workers began to grumble, then to complain, resist, and stage impromptu work stoppages, until finally they fled plant grounds, found sanctuary in local churches, contacted lawyers, and filed suits against crab processors for holding them in servitude.

It was population dynamics gone crazy. With the arrival of Mexican women, the balance of power that had existed between African-American women and crab-plant owners—seated in community-wide relations and the opportunities of household, family, and economy—had shifted, too far in favor of the processors.

In documents compiled for a lawsuit against two crab-plant owners—one in Maryland and another in North Carolina—fifteen Mexican women brought into the United States to pick crab claimed that their employers failed to pay them minimum wage, refused to pay overtime, housed them in subhuman conditions, and harassed them whenever they tried to leave the plant. The headline of a newspaper article covering the case read, "Women Held in Virtual Servitude," and several related stories chronicled accounts of abuse that confirm Saul Bellow's assertion that "ever since the Emancipation Proclamation people have been looking for new ways to invent slavery." Even Mary McGuire, who pioneered the use of foreign labor, deplored the way these two crab processors treated the women. How could they do such a thing? What compelled them to suspend their consciences and think they could get away with what amounted to modern slavery?

Presumably, because the plaintiffs were foreign women, apparently vulnerable, because they came from villages where five dollars a day was the prevailing wage, because they spoke little English and knew little about the system of justice in the United States, they would agree without argument or complaint to sleep two to a bed and work nights and weekends, or spend hours and days without any work at all, housed far down a dirt road or in the center of a town that had little more than two gas pumps and a convenience store.

Attitudes like these derive from the typical logic of those who employ immigrants: Used to squalid living conditions and hazardous, onerous working conditions in their home countries, immigrants should be happy to receive two dollars an hour, a roof, running water. Or, for every immigrant who gets a job in America, there are a hundred others clamoring at the border, hungry to fill their shoes. Or, I've been to their country, I've seen how they live.

I began interviewing employers of foreign workers fifteen years ago, speaking first with men and women in the Florida sugar industry and with apple growers from Virginia to Maine along the eastern seaboard. They hired the workers from Jamaica that helped propel Ralph Wallace into Mary McGuire's labor problems. It so happens that the Jamaican apple and sugarcane workers carried visas similar to those the Mexican women in the crab plants carry: "H" class visas, certifying foreign workers to perform temporary work in the United States. Ironically, "H" class visas are issued to people like Mick Jagger and Eric Clapton as well as top foreign heart surgeons or structural engineers—that is, people of exceptional talent and skill—when they come into the United States to perform their music or practice their craft. Such workers are considered temporary foreign workers according to U.S. immigration law. H-2 visas, by contrast, are issued to people who have no exceptional skills and who are willing to work in unpleasant jobs that few Americans are willing to perform. The H-2 visa, also unlike the H visas issued to rock stars, certifies a worker to work for a single employer and perform a single task. The Mexican women and Jamaican men brought in to work with such visas do not have free and unfettered access to the U.S. labor market.

H-2 visas have always been points of contention in Congress and within the government agencies—Labor and Immigration—involved in certifying industries and issuing the visas themselves. Internal debate over these visas can cause two offices inside the U.S. Department of Labor to dispute one another over the need for foreign labor. It was this kind of internal disagreement that led to the West Virginia case in which judges and senators supported local apple growers when a subdivision of the Department of Labor brought in Puerto Ricans to pick apples after another subdivision had authorized importing Jamaicans. The judges and the senators shared many of the growers' beliefs about immigrants: that they should be happy to stoop over 200-foot rows of cane, or reach to their muscle-straining lengths to pick apples at the ends of limbs, that however bad work and housing were here they would have been worse off where they came from.

After interviewing apple and sugar growers I moved on, over the years, to interviewing the personnel managers of chicken and turkey plants from Maryland to Texas, vegetable producers in southern Florida, peach growers in the Carolinas, and meatpacking plant personnel managers in Iowa, Minnesota, and Kansas. U.S. presidents and their appointed secretaries of labor and heads of the Immigration and Naturalization Service came and went. Senator Alan Simpson, a Republican from Wyoming, shepherded several immigration reform packages into the halls of Congress, finally introducing, defending, and witnessing President Bush sign into law the 1986 Immigration Reform and Control

Act. Federal immigration commissions flourished and faded away and flourished again. This was about the time that General Motors approached bankruptcy and IBM faltered, perhaps suggesting to more than a few statesmen that a little economic stimulant in the form of cheap immigrant labor was just what the country needed.

Throughout these years I kept interviewing. Employers of foreign workers sang the same songs, celebrating immigrants' working habits while justifying paying them less, working them harder, and controlling their lives through transportation and housing, drawing always on that diehard piece of comparative analysis: however depressed or depressing conditions of work and life are for immigrants here, they were far worse for immigrants at home.

Incidents leading to the lawsuit against the two crab-plant owners acted on ideas like these. In January 1991, after two years of successfully importing Mexican workers to his own plant in North Carolina, Conway Volstead, along with a Mexican crab picker turned labor contractor named Mona Cruz de Garzan, contacted Peter Hardaway about problems he was having finding crab pickers for his Maryland plant. Along with Mary McGuire and another crab picker in Oriental, North Carolina, Volstead was among the first crab-plant owners in the Mid-Atlantic region to experiment with Mexican labor. Unlike Mary McGuire and the plant owners in the town of Oriental, Volstead and Cruz established themselves as labor contractors. Recruiting Mexican women for their own as well as for others' plants, they asked only that those for whom they found Mexican pickers kicked back 10 cents for each pound of crabmeat each Mexican picked. Early in 1991, Peter Hardaway became one of their clients.

In May of that year, Volstead and Cruz traveled to Juan Jose Rios and Los Mochis in the Mexican state of Sinaloa, several hundred miles into Mexico from the U.S. border. Sinaloa is a state of industrialized food production, where fishing fleets and huge agricultural fields provide a wide array of land and sea products, including blue crabs, to packing and shipping plants lining the Inter-American Highway. Los Mochis, a large city of around 200,000, serves as a commercial center for several large U.S. and Mexican agricultural firms, many with names familiar to people living in the U.S. Midwest. Juan Jose Rios is one of a series of small, much poorer, ramshackle communities to the south of Los Mochis, which seem to be built on an infrastructure of scavenged wood, hope, and scrap metal. They supply workers to the huge farms and packing operations that line the highway and serve as centers where workers learn, often from a very young age, the rigors of workplace discipline and the unpredictability of seasonal, hazardous jobs. They are nurseries for workers who grow up to work in places like the gladiolus fields of southern Florida, the tomato fields of Pennsylvania, or the crab-picking plants of the Mid-Atlantic Coast.

Volstead and Cruz traveled to Sinaloa to entice fifteen young women to work for Peter Hardaway through the summer. Once there, they portrayed the jobs at Hardaway's plant as fairly highpaying, showing them pay stubs of crab pickers who had made $250 a week, and bringing in Mexican women who had worked in Volstead's plant to testify that everything Volstead and Cruz told them was true. Two hundred fifty dollars a week. Living on Maryland's lovely eastern shore. Shopping excursions on weekends. They were guaranteed work, transportation, housing with air-conditioning, television, and laundry facilities.

Volstead and Cruz helped the fifteen women who agreed to pick crabs through the paperwork of passports and visas and put them on a bus to Maryland. Within three weeks of Volstead's and Cruz's first visits to Los Mochis and Juan Jose Rios, on May 18, 1991, they stepped off a bus in the tiny town of Secretary, Maryland, met their new boss and his Spanish-speaking foreman, a man named Comachilla, and saw where they would be staying over the next six to eight months. Their living quarters were disappointing. In Mexico, Volstead and Cruz promised them that only four women would occupy a single bedroom. In Maryland, that first day, according to documents presented in U.S. District Court, "they were given a choice of two different sets of living quarters: a small one bedroom / one bathroom house and an adjacent three bedroom house. Twelve of the plaintiffs lived in the one bedroom house; five women slept in the bedroom, three slept on cots set up in the upstairs hallway, and five slept in the living room. The remaining three plaintiffs, together with eight other migrant workers . . . and defendant Comachilla, lived in the three bedroom house. Comachilla, his wife and sister slept in one bedroom; each of the remaining two bedrooms was occupied by five women."

The first few days at Hardaway's plant opened many of the Mexican women's eyes to what lay ahead in terms of work, leisure, and earnings. Their living accommodations were only the first of several disappointments. With Comachilla translating, Peter Hardaway traced the boundaries of the plant and told them they were to respect these boundaries as if they were the U.S.-Mexico border. Telling them he feared for their safety, he said they shouldn't walk around town at night. In fact, he said, it probably wouldn't be wise to leave the plant premises without permission.

During the first week at Hardaway's, these recommendations solidified into rules. Several of the women took to lingering at the end of a nearby dock during their time off, chatting and giggling and sipping beer and soft drinks, trying to make the most of otherwise difficult conditions. Unfortunately, Hardaway's neighbors complained. The town of Secretary, Maryland, has fewer than 1,000 persons. This region of Maryland boasts an ambivalent heritage that combines North and South, Blue and Gray, situated midway between Norfolk and Philadelphia— the former a seat of racism, the latter a city founded on liberty and at one time the heart of the abolitionist movement. Natives of Maryland's eastern shore express this ambivalence, today, in the mixed feelings that many Americans harbor toward immigrants and immigration.

It is said William Faulkner once remarked that Northerners love the black race but despise the black individual, while Southerners love the black individual but hate the black race. Toward immigrants, especially immigrants of color, from Mexico, Central America, and the Caribbean, Americans tend to adopt the Southern perspective. We adore the Jamaican waiter, with his British accent and manners, and we very nearly adopt the Guatemalan or Dominican domestic servant, but we look with less heart, less compassion, on the teeming masses at Ellis Island or, more appropriate today, the fleets of makeshift rafts full of Haitians approaching Florida. Most Americans love individual immigrants but despise immigration.

Communities along Maryland's eastern shore, at least since the early 1980s, had been experiencing increased influxes of immigrants from Mexico, Central America, and the Caribbean because of the region's chicken factories and vegetable farms. I once asked the personnel manager of a Maryland poultry company if he had trouble finding workers for his plants and he said, "We were having a difficult time finding labor four, four-and-a-half years ago. We had to get innovative. We sent screeners down to Indiantown, Florida, and began recruiting Guatemalans. They all worked in agriculture. At first we housed them in the old motels along Route 13, but after a while they matriculated into the community. They help each other out."

He actually used the word "matriculated," a word similar to the Spanish word meaning "registered for college classes." This personnel manager was not referring to school enrollment, though, but rather to the predictable process by which ethnically similar immigrants assist one another with housing, transportation, and information, gradually building up a presence in the community.

To the residents of the town of Secretary who complained about the Mexican women, the desire to keep the women inside Hardaway's plant might well have stemmed from the recent growth of Latino immigrants on Maryland's eastern shore. In most such communities, new immigrants tend to be viewed as somehow frightening, threatening, transient, unfamiliar, and strange, lacing local customs with foreign dialects and malodorous foods. Stories reflecting Americans' fears of new immigrants are common. When Southeast Asians began moving into Washington, D.C., neighborhoods, residents complained that they were losing their dogs and cats to the refugees' stir-fry and stew. Native Miamians complain that there are no longer any English-speaking radio stations in the city, yet English radio programming outnumbers Spanish programming by a ratio of more than two to one. In Detroit in the 1920s, when blacks began streaming into the city at a rate of more than thirty a day, a prominent black physician moved into his home in a mainly white neighborhood under police protection and, two days later, woke to angry whites throwing rocks through his windows.

Whether seated in uneasy race relations or merely everyday xenophobia, the apprehensions natives have about new immigrants are as predictable as sunsets. No one should have been surprised when longtime residents of Secretary complained about the mere presence of Mexican women, but Hardaway's response to the complaints was exaggerated to a degree that even most of his fellow plant owners disapproved of. First he confiscated the passports, visas, and work permits of the Mexican women, converting them into illegal aliens whenever they weren't near him. Then he essentially imprisoned them. They weren't slaves exactly, weren't shackled to their beds or locked inside the plant, but Hardaway confined them to the plant unless he or someone in a supervisory position accompanied them. Thus, when they left the plant it was similar to the way prison road crews leave minimum security prisons, escorted and watched.

But with the same subtle charms of resistance that the African-American women used when plant owners tried to coerce them into coming into the plants, a few of the Mexican women under Hardaway's thumb wriggled free. Keep in mind that these were young women, most around the age of twenty-five, who would not submit to being treated like either slaves or children any more than the young African-American women in Pamlico County who stopped applying for crab-picking jobs would. One day, while shopping during one of their accompanied excursions, they met a few Spanish-speaking men, who picked them up at the plant one night and drove them to Washington, D.C., for what the court report called "a night on the town."

The next day, a Sunday in late June, Hardaway summoned the women to his office, told them he knew about the outing to Washington, and again stressed that they were not to leave the plant premises without someone from the plant accompanying them. At least two of the women challenged Hardaway's authority then and there, leaving the meeting before Hardaway was finished. They had, they said, social engagements elsewhere. They drove off into Maryland's Sunday afternoon with some of the men from the previous evening.

That, according to Hardaway, was the last straw. He called Volstead and Cruz to Maryland to threaten the women with the principal threat employers of immigrants use against them: deportation. Essentially, they threaten them with home. What is so threatening about home? Immigrants often pin greater hopes than they perhaps should to migrating for work in the United States. But because enough immigrants return from the United States with fancy clothes, jewelry, watches, and often money to invest in housing and land, most of those who emigrate do so carrying high expectations of similar triumphant returns. When they return without the things of successful migrants, having been fired, they return in shame.

Cruz's threats against the women, however, were even more potentially devastating: she threatened to send them back to Mexico, but not to their home villages. She said that she and Volstead would drop them off just across the border, without money or documents, anywhere from six to twelve hours from home. To reach Los Mochis and Juan Jose Rios—the two native villages where Cruz and Volstead recruited them—they would have to negotiate with drivers for free rides across miles and miles of Mexico's interior.

Cruz's visit was not entirely hostile. She tried her best to calm the women about the terms of their employment by explaining, painstakingly, the various deductions Hardaway listed on their pay stubs. They did not dispute the charges for travel and rent, at least not with Cruz, and perhaps they drew some small comfort from the explanations. Paternalism is often like that, and the way Hardaway, Volstead, and Cruz interacted with the young women was paternal through and through. Cruel yet at times benevolent, it was an imbalanced mixture of the routine cruelty of long hours at the picking tables and close supervision of work and leisure, with occasional small gifts of shopping excursions, calming explanations about pay, and promises of higher earnings once they paid off their travel expenses and the crab season picked up.

For some workers, these occasional pats on the back were enough.

But others questioned working conditions and payment systems at the plant. Others grew increasingly dissatisfied with the gouged paychecks and rules about not leaving the plant. Over the week following Cruz's visit, these unhappy crab pickers got word of their circumstances to a lawyer in Washington D.C., a woman who had worked closely with various legal service organizations up and down the eastern seaboard and who no doubt knew the faces of the powerless all too well. Within days of Cruz's visit, on the morning of July 6, another visitor showed up at Hardaway's plant: Martha Ames, an investigator for the wage-and-hour division of the Maryland Department of Labor and Industry. Investigator Ames immediately spotted several irregularities in the way Hardaway paid the Mexican women, including failure to pay minimum hourly wages and overtime and, not surprising, deducting for expenses without the written permission of the workers. She added that Hardaway had no legal right to keep the workers' passports and other travel documents.

After Ames's visit, tensions at the plant escalated quickly. Hardaway, fearing fines from the wage-and-hour division, began interrogating people in the plant and soon learned that some of the workers had contacted someone, "possibly a lawyer," about their working conditions. That afternoon, only hours after Investigator Ames's departure, Hardaway called all the Mexican women to his office and began shouting at them. The bilingual foreman, Comachilla, also from Mexico, translated, telling the women that those who had contacted the lawyer would have to leave the plant. Anyone else who didn't like conditions at the plant, he yelled, should leave too: in the morning he would put them all on a bus to Mexico.

The women spent a long night at Hardaway's plant. Those who had chosen to leave packed their bags, their emotions brimming, and many of the others were too distressed to sleep. A long, depressing night. While the women at Hardaway's consoled one another, Mona Cruz drove north across northeastern North Carolina, passing through the Great Dismal Swamp and crossing the Chesapeake Bay Bridge Tunnel, arriving at Hardaway's plant on the morning of July 7 to salvage what was left of the labor force. Volstead was behind this. He wanted the 10 cents per pound of crabmeat per worker that Hardaway mailed to him after each pay period. Cruz showed up to repeat the threats she had made earlier, but by the time Cruz arrived lawyers from a legal assistance corporation in Washington had arrived too. Also attending the tension was an FBI agent and several men who worked for Hardaway and who, as the day progressed, began drinking and surrounding the women's residences.

Sometime late in the day, as threats against the women became more virulent, the lawyers decided to move the women to a safer location, taking them into Washington to a women's shelter called Luther Place. There they remained for three weeks, until Hardaway and two men who worked for him decided to try to pressure them into signing forms that would release Hardaway from any legal claims against him. Showing up at Luther Place at 2:00 A.M., Hardaway and the two men threw a rock through the shelter's window, demanding that the Mexican women come out and sign the forms.

As a woman's shelter, Luther Place was used to dealing with unruly men. Typically these shelters secure themselves against angry boyfriends and husbands who view girlfriends and wives as their property. Hardaway could not have been much different from the men the shelter was used to, given his attempt to confine the women to plant premises and his presumption, at Luther Place, that he could order them into the street with stones. The women of Luther Place called the police, and when they arrived they encountered a scene resembling a domestic dispute: Hardaway shouting, the women crying, Hardaway demanding that the women return to the plant or sign the release forms, the women refusing and seeking protection from their sisters in the shelter. Only after the police threatened to charge Hardaway with kidnapping did the physical dimensions of this prolonged labor dispute finally end.

A little over two years later, a district court judge ruled that Hardaway had treated the women unfairly and that Cruz and Volstead had conspired with Hardaway to pay them less than minimum wage, and ordered Hardaway to pay back wages. Shortly thereafter, Hardaway closed down his plant and sold out. Volstead remained in business.

What happened at Hardaway's plant was the result of imbalance, of the environmental conditions favoring one group over another to a point where either the weak disappear or the strong go berserk with power. We've seen this occur with carp, starlings, zebra mussels, and the weeds and grasses that choke our waters after overloadings of nutrients. Mexican nationals and immigrants in general, working in the U.S. labor market, operate from a position of weakness. In a rural legal aid office in Immokalee, Florida, I once spent days and days sifting through court cases, depositions, and testimonies about incidents as bad or worse than the Hardaway case. Men murdered for disputing their paychecks or abandoned in shallow graves after pesticide poisoning. People chained to their cots at night, starved for not working hard enough, or pistol-whipped for trying to leave labor camps at night. These are the perverse consequences of an imbalance of powers grown so acute that those with the advantage lose sight of the give-and-take of human relationships. In short, they lose sight of the sense of the gift that always lurks somewhere, even if in vestigial form, behind the agreements between employees and employers regarding fair work and fair pay.

A simple statement by Mary McGuire, one of the pioneers of the Mexican connection, shows that not all crab-plant owners have adopted the attitudes and practices of the few Volsteads and Hardaways that taint labor relations with their selfishness. When we spoke about the growing use of Mexican women in the crab houses, it was McGuire, not I, who raised the issue of the Hardaway case, stepping back from her interests as an employer and a crab-plant owner and joining, for a moment, a community of the generous and humane, commenting, "I think it's terrible the way Hardaway treated those poor girls."

FISHING

IN

THE

BALANCE

We were sitting in an office with a view of Houston's skyline, twenty-two floors up, sipping coffee from delicate china cups. At his walnut desk, Arnie Roth sorted cards illustrated with drawings of fish into piles. I had asked Arnie to group the fish according to how he believed they were similar. "Use any criteria you want," I said. "I can't suggest anything. It might influence your thinking."

Arnie was a kind man, large and white-haired, in his late fifties, a gracious host, and one of the top executives in a company that owned parking garages and lots in major cities throughout the United States. He sorted the pictures of fish in a typical manner—"These are good to eat, these fun to catch, these you catch closer to shore"—making offhand comments about individual fish such as "Pompano will come into shore, but mainly they stay out in the open ocean" or "You catch these big gag grouper when you bottom fish around wrecks."

After I recorded his ideas about fish and put away the cards, I asked him a standard series of questions about his fishing experiences. How long had he fished recreationally? What percentage of his fishing effort was done from shore? From a boat? What kind of boat? We ended the formal portion of the interview with the required demographics: age, family size, education, and so on. He smiled at the question about income; our highest income bracket was "more than $40,000 per year."

Considerably more, I suspected. He owned a yacht and fished in tournaments with entry fees in the thousands and purses in the hundreds of thousands. He paid dues to an organization that adopted redfish as a symbol and claimed to have saved them from the brink of extinction by banning commercial redfish landings in Texas and beginning a hatchery program. He mentioned Marlin fishing off the coast of Cancun and described in sumptuous detail how various hardwood chips added to smokers flavored the meat of cobia and pompano. When I left, I felt grateful that someone so advanced along the executive ladder, so high above Houston's skyline, had granted me nearly an hour of his time.

Similar experiences followed. I spent ten days in Houston interviewing recreational fishers, leaving my cheap motel two blocks from the Astrodome to ride elevators into executive suites or to cross yards of soft carpeting into the plush private quarters of physicians and attorneys. For four months I replicated these experiences in Daytona Beach, Tampa, Raleigh, and eastern North Carolina. I was invited onto sportfishing vessels that cost $1,000 just to fill with gas. I attended captains' banquets during sportfishing tournaments and sampled from huge spreads of cocktail shrimp, backfin crab cakes, and scallops wrapped in bacon. One angler met me at the door of his mansion and led me into a den with a wall of stuffed heads—the most prominent a giraffe's, its neck curving upward into a gabled and glassed ceiling from a brass and cherrywood plaque.

It was quite a time. Never before had I experienced such opulence mixed with such concern over the health of the fishes of the sea. At times, interviewing the presidents of sportfishing clubs, I felt as though I had strayed into the offices of Green Peace or the Sierra Club. One common thread ran through these interviews: there was little doubt in most of these anglers' minds who constituted the most despicable enemy of fish and oceans. When they prefaced their speeches about environmental protection and conservation with rhetorical musing about who might be most responsible for ruining substrates, damaging reefs, and for the precipitous decline in fish populations worldwide, I wondered, at first, Who? Toxic waste disposal firms? Oil companies, with their offshore drilling and spilling? Resort developers draining wetlands to erect condominiums and hotels? Or those who backed bond offerings to build dams, dikes, jetties, and other barriers to the annual migrations of fish?

No, they assured me. None of those. Instead, all fingers pointed in one direction, all blame settled on one highly visible population that forever frustrated the navigational desires and leisure time of these recreational anglers, these sportsmen and yachtsmen: nearly everyone of them pointed their fingers at commercial fishers. These recreational anglers spoke about commercial fishers as though they were trolls snatching babies from the deep, vampires sucking the waters of their lifebloods, environmental rapists surrounding porpoises with nets and drowning turtles in tangles of otter trawls.

If at first I dutifully recorded these comments, nodding, gradually I began noticing that they quoted many of the same sources and repeated the party-line proclamations of sportfishing club newsletters. And I began considering their sources. Arnie Roth, for example, the kind white-haired gentleman who served me coffee high above Houston's skyline, was in the business of parking lots. He managed concrete highrises that accommodated people who clogged expressways with automobiles, injuring the atmosphere with carbon monoxide. He paved paradise, in Bob Dylan's words, and put up a parking lot.

Arnie was not alone. The membership rosters of sportfishing clubs were crowded with the names of men who hunted endangered species, drained wetlands to build condominiums, and thought nothing of catching more bluefish and king mackerel than they could ever consume. They were quick to blame commercial fishers for declines in fish stocks, yet slow to recognize how their own consumption behaviors and positions as company executives might stress the natural world. They be-

Recreational fishers, Shackleford Banks, c. 1920

lieved in the seemingly obvious yet biologically shaky proposition that overfishing was the primary cause of the decline of fish around the world. Typically, several claims about the economic benefits of sportfishing accompanied this proposition: sportfishing clubs sponsored the sinking of boxcars to create new artificial reefs, and sportfishers themselves stimulated employment and revenues for coastal areas through what economists call multiplier effects. Some economists went so far as to suggest that the entire coastal tourist industry was built up on a substrate of angling.

The joke that North Carolina commercial fishers repeat in response to this assertion is, "Sportfishers come to the coast with a clean shirt and a twenty dollar bill and they don't change either one."

Behind these quips and arguments lie serious questions about rights to the resource. Any fishery social scientist—whether economist, sociologist, or anthropologist—is quick to point out that oceans, rivers, lakes, and most other bodies of water are common property resources: beyond private ownership, they are owned and managed by the state or by some governing body that transcends an individual or even a family. Like public parks, they exist for the good of all members of a nation or community, often deeply entangled in national and community heritage. Indeed, many common property resources—think of the Liberty Bell, Yellowstone Park, the Washington Monument, or even the statue of the bear in the yard of the high school in Bear Grass, North Carolina— enable us to imagine ourselves to be members of a nation or community in the first place, a people linked by similar dreams, hopes, foods, symbols, and fears.

Common properties used to be far more widespread than they are today. Before Columbus, many of the indigenous peoples who lived in the western hemisphere held rights to land and water communally, in groups of large, extended families who shared ethnic myths about human origins, passed remedies for illness down through the generations, and repeated oral histories about their ancestors. Shepherds of biblical times viewed many of the pastures and oases where they grazed and watered their livestock as commons, open to all who shared in the visions of Israelites or Bedouins. Until the recent wars and terrors in Iran, the Bakhtari moved flocks of sheep and goats between summer highlands and winter lowlands, laying tribal claim to pastures and wateringholes seasonally, but leaving them for others during the remainder of the year.

Access to most common property resources is usually constrained or mediated somehow, by rights of birth or heritage or by the watchful eyes of councils, commissions, governments. One of the best-known writers about common property resources was Garret Hardin, whose article on the tragedy of the commons has become the conventional wisdom of many fisheries economists, sociologists, and anthropologists yet has emerged as the theoretical whipping-boy of the more astute of these fields.

Hardin's thesis, briefly, is that open access to any commons will result in its destruction: individuals benefit by taking as much out of the resource as they can while investing little energy or expense in keeping the resource healthy. The classic example of this is our use and abuse of the world's air supply. While everyone benefits from clean air, those nations, companies, and individuals who pollute the air more than others do not pay any more or less for their actions than any other living, breathing thing. Benefits accrue to individuals, but costs are distributed over the whole earth.

Hardin's thesis makes a good deal of sense among people who champion individual rights so much that they find nothing pretentious about naming entire bodies of water after themselves. But it makes less sense when we consider common property resources in local settings, where communities and neighborhoods depend on those resources to survive. Day-to-day, regular interactions and exchanges of greetings, gifts, and marriage partners between neighbors has a way of tempering the greed and selfishness on which Hardin's thesis depends. This is especially true when an individual's selfish behavior threatens the very resource—be it air, water, fish, game, grazing land, or whatever—that a neighborhood or community needs for its continued well-being.

Those social and cultural analysts who pay close attention to small groups in local settings find fault with Hardin's thesis because Hardin assumes that the selfishness that leads a company to pollute a stream also characterizes people with traditions of gift exchange, cooperation, and the conservation of natural resources. Anthropologists find Hardin's assumptions extremely ethnocentric, because he is judging people all around the world by the moral values and practical standards of his own culture. Sociologists and economists could easily criticize Hardin's thesis for failing to consider the values of social and cultural capital—forms of capital that benefit entire communities—relative to the value that an individual receives from overexploiting a resource. Nevertheless, Hardin and his proponents apply the conventional wisdom of Western corporate economics to people who do not plan their activities according to quarterly profit cycles or the accumulation of wealth for its own sake. Even Western societies have moral mechanisms to temper selfishness and encourage gift-giving and cooperation. Would we continue to repeat parables of sharing and altruism if this were not so? Would any of us know the story of the mother hen who bakes bread or repeat the Golden Rule? Would we wage prolonged political struggles against lumbering in Yellowstone Park or oil exploration in Alaska's last wilderness? In small, meaningful groups, where all identity ultimately resides—in families and neighborhoods, regions and communities—we are neither selfish nor acquisitive, but open, sharing, and giving.

But we need not assess Hardin's thesis based on principle alone. Exemplary cases of folk conservation practices are found throughout the literature about cultures whose members depend heavily on intimate links with nature. My friend and colleague, Bonnie McCay, an anthropologist at Rutgers University's Human Ecology Department, co-edited a book entitled *The Question of the Commons* with James Acheson of the University of Maine. The collection brought together the work of nineteen social scientists around the question of communal resources and Hardin's assumptions of selfishness and environmental destruction. They described folk conservation practices in regions as widely separated as New Guinea and the Canadian subarctic, finding people who conserved common property resources in places as near to Wall Street as the coast of Maine and as foreign to the principles of Western economics as the Cocamilla of the Amazon Basin. Working among lobstermen of Maine, for example, Acheson found that harbor gangs defined and laid claim to lobstering territories, limiting access to them based on longtime residence in the community and kinship or friendship ties to elder lobstermen. They maintained territorial boundaries with methods ranging from direct confrontations to the clandestine cutting or sinking of a trespasser's traps. These practices limited the number of individuals in each lobstering ground, while pressuring those within each territory to limit the number of traps they set, aiding in the conservation of lobster stocks.

Folk conservation rarely occurs for the sake of subsistence or economic integrity alone. Cultural identity also encourages people to conserve natural resources, lacing environmental practices with feelings of self worth. What people *receive* from natural resources—a sense of belonging, a sense of place—is what encourages people to give back the gift of conserving those resources. Rarely do people conserving natural resources forgo the possibility of making a living from them, but sometimes just making a living, subsisting, is about all they can be said to be doing. I have visited fishing families from Maine to Puerto Rico without once encountering the opulence and conspicuous consumption I encountered while interviewing recreational anglers in Texas, Florida, and North Carolina. In the cases assembled together in Acheson and McCay's book, people demonstrated a meaningful attachment to resources they considered local, resources that benefited neighbors, friends, and members of their communities. These resources were part of their heritage, their local history, their stores of wealth that could not be priced, bought, or sold, but instead entered into their body of well-being similar to the way people give and receive gifts.

The Chisasibi Cree Indians who fish, hunt, and trap in and around the Hudson Bay in Quebec view the land and water of their territory simply as within their responsibility or under their stewardship, belonging not to an individual or even the tribe, but to their God. In the Amazon Basin, a widespread Cocamilla taboo against fishing for dolphins serves to maintain the integrity of the food chain, because taking so large a creature out of the balance of predator-prey relationships might disrupt the entire chain. Thus, the beliefs of the Cocamilla and their fishing and conservation practices become intimately intertwined, drawing the natural environment into their sense of who they are. Conserving natural resources that have historically served as sources of cultural identity, of a people's or society's sense of self and worth, nearly always takes precedence over the narrow rewards of profit. Current debates over proposals to mine or drill for oil in our national parks demonstrate that, even in societies that cherish principles of accumulation and profit, some natural resources are too dear to our heritage to place within the reach of corporate greed.

The cultural identity and heritage that encourage conserving natural resources, handed down through generations and along lifetimes of experience, develop hand in hand with close, repeated observations of one's environment that are informed by a vast accumulated store of folk knowledge about that environment. The ways people add to and revise this knowledge are sometimes straightforward and direct, yet sometimes mystical and difficult to trace, taking place in those realms of human consciousness where intelligence mingles with wisdom. Among the fishers of the Mid-Atlantic Coast, this occurs on a nearly daily and often subliminal basis. This is not to say that the teachers and students of folk knowledge about estuaries, rivers, and sounds take this knowledge for granted. A single day spent with a man on a skiff pulling a scallop dredge near Harker's Island, or working a string of eel and crab pots in Albemarle Sound, a late winter afternoon consumed by a long conversation with a man who descends from twelve generations of fishers, or an evening's discussion among a small, intimate gathering of fishers—any of these will reveal the security and pride that fishers derive from the folk knowledge that guides their craft.

On a day of periodic cloudbursts followed by sudden clearing and intense sunlight in September, I visited Billy Gray, a fisherman in his middle thirties, bearded, windburned like most fishers, to begin a series of conversations about landing blue crabs and netting flounder. His wife and his son's future mother-in-law wove nets in a trailer across a small yard and work space from the trailer in which he lived. They make their home along the north shore of Albemarle Sound, 10 miles south of Elizabeth City, on Frog Island, where twenty or so fishers stack crab pots and launch skiffs.

The first time we met, Billy stepped out of the trailer where they wove nets, back from a morning's fishing, and spoke with me near his workshop beside a canal. In colonial times Elizabeth City traded with cities to the north by means of the Great Dismal Swamp Canal. On this narrower canal, Billy and his wife live in a row of fishing shacks and trailers, the yards fitted with docks and networks of pipes and basins that hold peeling and soft-shelled crabs. Beside these holding pens stands a workshop where monofilament line, cork, paints, lubricants of all kinds, and spare machine parts and tools seem to have achieved an uneasy balance for the sole principle of being within reach. It is unlikely, today, that the state would allow the dredging of a canal of this kind, a 300-yard channel that gives a dozen fishing families sheltered access to Albemarle Sound, but canal construction permits were among the least of Billy's worries about the state.

He spoke, instead, of a disturbing trend in the population of striped bass, one of the most important fishes in Albemarle and Currituck Sounds and in the Chesapeake Bay. Striped bass, locally known as rock or rockfish, are anadramous fishes, spending their lives moving between freshwater and saltwater environments, migrating into the open ocean during most of their lives yet coming inland to spawn like herring or salmon. In the open ocean, striped bass can reach lengths of up to 6 feet and weigh between 50 and 60 pounds. Farther inland, inside North Carolina's and Virginia's estuaries and swimming up great rivers like the Chowan, the Rappahannock, the James, and the Roanoke, striped bass spawn and feed on blue crabs and other fish and shellfish of the brackish and fresh waters of the estuaries.

Striped bass have long been important fish along the areas of North Carolina's coast that were first settled by Europeans moving south out of Jamestown, Virginia, as pioneers, cutting small farms and livestock pens out of the wilderness. Among the earliest photographs taken in North Carolina are those showing sport fishers around the turn of the century, outfitted with oilcloth hip-waders, bamboo poles with primitive reels leaning nearby, hefting striped bass lengthwise, the big fish stretching between two men. Other early photos show charter boats moored at Manteo docks after the passengers have changed into straw hats and summer suits to stand side by side behind stringers of scores of striped bass.

More recently, striped bass have been the subject of some of today's most sophisticated aquaculture research and at the heart of political disputes about the uses of water. My good friend Margie Gallagher, an aquaculture scientist of international renown, has experimented with enhanced feeds that enable striped bass to grow faster and larger than ever before. Another friend and colleague, Roger Rulifson, collected comprehensive data on striped bass for several years, in North Carolina and Nova Scotia, and once he had to have police protection to speak out against power companies whose construction activities interfered with rockfish migrations and spawning habits.

Thus, striped bass lie at the heart of several controversies regarding the estuary's gifts. The writing and revising of striped bass biographies in hatcheries and ponds, in rivers and sounds, stimulate debates between commercial and recreational fishers, arguments over natural resources versus urban development, and the future of fisheries in aquaculture, whose development encourages corporate creep into fisheries and reduces biological diversity, similar to monocropping in agriculture. Billy Gray's complaint was not so much about preserving striped bass stocks or seeing to their reproductive requirements in artificial environments, but about their abundance. For several years before I spoke with Billy, North Carolina restricted commercial landings of striped bass, reserving them for recreational fishers and allowing commercial fishers like Billy to catch only five a day, and those five only as a percentage of by-catch.

Billy's complaint, repeated by several other commercial fishers in Albemarle Sound, was that the commercial fishers had been removed from the chain of predator-prey relationships. Striped bass populations were growing too rapidly and, in the words of a fisherman from Columbia, across the Albemarle from Billy, "We're trying to fish around them."

One late afternoon and evening in March, six months after I first met Billy Gray, I drove along the shore of Albemarle to talk with fishers from Frog Island to Edenton on the north shore and from Columbia to the mouth of the Roanoke along the south shore. My first stop of the evening was Billy's, where I met with Billy, his son Miles, and a former crew member on Billy's boat who has since become a farmer, a young man named Roly. For two hours we drank whiskey and swapped fish stories for stories about the bureaucratic mess over fisheries in the state legislature.

We stood around a stack of freshly made eel pots inside Billy and Miles's workshop, a garage-like structure beside the two slips where they moor their boats. I leaned against a greasy work counter littered with rubber seals and washers below a pegboard holding wrenches, drills, pliers, drop cords, and all the other tools necessary to keep their vessels afloat, their crab and eel pots replenished, their motors tuned. You find these work spaces near the homes of commercial fishing families all along the Mid-Atlantic Coast. Everywhere they are the linchpin between the fishing family's social and natural worlds, the hinge where land and water meet. Cluttered, functional, preventive, even defensive, they focus the family's effort to check the natural deterioration of wood, wire, rubber, glass, and cork subjected daily to water, salt, and wind. When nails tremble, keels split, or surfaces flake at every touch, it is into these work spaces that they are taken, analyzed, discarded, recycled, or repaired. From shacks, barns, and garages like Billy's originated the sweeping juniper keel of the shad boat and the distinctive wide-bodied, open-decked vessel from which crabbers set their pots.

It was the first week of March. In less than a month the herring would begin to boil into the Albemarle, and after the herring began tapering off it would be time to set crab and eel pots. All through summer, their peak season, they would be hauling hundreds of pots daily, sorting the large and small jimmies and sooks into separate piles and carefully placing the peelers into basins of circulating water until they shed their outer skeletons and became the high-priced soft-shell crabs. But this first week of March was a slow time for them, the end of a slow winter of fishing that had become slower because of the abundance of striped bass.

Miles was quiet, but Billy and Roly, loosening up with the whiskey, became increasingly irate over the current trends in the fisheries. At the time, I was collecting information for a state committee that would soon propose new regulations to the state legislature. After seeing the direction in which the committee was headed, the backs being scratched, the favors being repaid, the yes-men bureaucrats and researchers saying whatever they were told to say, I was as dismayed with the political process as most of the fishers and their families. At one committee meeting, I made the seemingly innocuous comment that commercial fishers observed and monitored the resource through the year day in and day out and that regulating them off the water would upset the balance of predator and prey. For saying this, the committee chairman took steps to have me screened and censored before future presentations, yet the commercial fishers I met over the next few weeks shook my hand and said things like "Finally someone is saying something good about commercial fishermen."

Why this contradiction? The answer lies in the frustration of men like Billy Gray over issues like the population of striped bass. In 1991, the state enacted rules about striped bass that essentially classified this fish as a sportfish, restricting the number, times of year, and areas where you could catch striped bass to sell. This fish that for centuries had a dual personality, both a commercial and recreational fish, lost one of its main predators.

We saw what happened in the blue-crab industry when the Department of Labor overstocked the labor market with unsuspecting Mexican women: the population dynamics went crazy, favoring the processing-plant owners to such a degree that they began treating these immigrant women like indentured servants, deducting exorbitant rents from their weekly paychecks as in the days of debt peonage. Likewise in the North Sea, when well-intentioned environmentalists protected baby seals from gruesome slaughter by fur hunters, seal populations increased so dramatically that they feasted on fish stocks along the Scandinavian coast, outstripped the food supply, and starved to death in great numbers.

Beginning in 1991, with commercial fishers legally removed from an effective role in the chain of predator-prey relationships, striped bass stocks began growing. By 1995 they had become so thick that they clogged flounder nets and began threatening the blue-crab population. In March of 1996, biologists opened up a striped bass and found in its stomach more than forty blue crabs, a favorite food not only of striped bass but also of redfish and several other species that sportfishers have moved to protect. About this, Carl Murphy of Stumpy Point said:

> It killed at least forty-one crabs, that one fish. And I come home that Sunday and I wrote on my little piece of paper in longhand figures, that if one rock eats forty-one crabs a day for a year, and

there were in our North Carolina waters two million—I think this is a real conservative estimate about how many rock we have, since you can catch rock in our area anywhere you drop a hook. . . . And if two million is close, and forty-one is accurate, then in a year the rock would eat, it seems like, around three trillion crabs. . . . There's about three hundred twenty-five crabs to one hundred pounds. According to my longhand figures, [those crabs would make] about nine-hundred billion pounds of crab. The fishery estimated they caught forty-three million pounds three or four years ago. Last year was fifty-three million. This [the nine-hundred billion] is probably more crabs would be eaten in one year than's been caught in North Carolina by crabpotters since the beginning of tagging. If Adam had of been a crabpotter, they wouldn't have caught that many crabs by now.

Again, we have population dynamics gone crazy. And again, the unbalanced environment, thick with striped bass, encouraged behaviors as corrupt and perverse as those of the processing-plant owners who imprisoned, underpaid, and overcharged young immigrant women. The chief gripes of Billy and Roly were directed toward fishing practices that emerged in the aftermath of the thickening of striped bass populations. First, some fishers were indiscriminately killing thousands of pounds of striped bass to land a few hundred pounds of flounder. To Billy, and to other fishers whose lives revolved around the rhythms of the Albemarle, this waste of the estuary's gifts was unnatural and even immoral. It was driven, he understood, by the market, the quest for profit, but neither Billy nor his son Miles could bear to kill, needlessly, so many striped bass for a smaller amount of flounder.

The second perverse practice that the thickening of striped bass encouraged was the reentry into the fishery of men who had quit fishing, who had full-time jobs on the shore yet came back to fish because catching striped bass had become nearly as easy as dip-netting herring during the spring runs. Speaking of one of these failed, returning fishers, Roly said, "He couldn't catch clap in a whorehouse, but he can catch striped bass. Hell, anybody can catch striped bass." Like canned hunting, where hunters kill penned animals, fishers without any fishing skills— Billy's neighbors—were coming home after work, puttering out into the sound, catching five striped bass, puttering home to put them in the freezer, leaving again to catch another five, coming home and going out again and again into the evening.

If selective pressures drove these fishers off the water years earlier, the overabundance of striped bass drew them back onto the water. Later that evening, after leaving Billy, Roly, and Miles, I met with seven other fishermen and their wives to discuss the proposed regulations and the problems they were experiencing. One of them, a tall, thin man named Gabe Bishop, a fisherman/farmer whose family had been landing herring for three generations, said:

> It's crazier right now than I've ever seen, and I've been around fishing all my life. But right now you can set one thousand yards of net. So you pull out a thousand yards of net, you get halfway down, and you've got five rock. You look at them and put them in the boat, and you pull a little farther and there's one bigger. So you take one of them and you flip him out and you lay another down. You're killing rock all the way down.

The others at the meeting nodded in agreement or shook their heads to share in Gabe's disgust, and a younger fisherman than Gabe, Benny Ormond, moved a plug of tobacco aside, pushed back his bright orange cap, and added, "You're killing rock, killing rock, killing rock. And that's what this whole business is about, killing rock. They've got the worst law in place for restoring rock that they could have."

Yet the laws keep coming, piling regulation on regulation, layering rules like coats of paint over the antique woodwork of fishing practices dating back centuries. A thick, impenetrable book about the size of Mao Tse Tung's red book contains all the regulations dictating the dos and don'ts of fishing; these are supplemented by almost daily mailings from the director of the Division of Marine Fisheries called "Proclamations."

On top of these are licenses: vessel licenses, licenses to fish, licenses to sell fish, gear licenses, licenses to operate a facility to clean and pack fish, and so on. Of these Gabe said, with an exasperated tone:

> Good God Almighty! My pocketbook won't hold the cards I have to take to get into the river. I ain't lying. You almost need a satchel along with you to put the amount of plastic that they give you to be able to sell something. . . . For God's sake, let them do *one* thing, let them come out with one license that a full-time commercial fisherman can buy for a certain price and it covers *everything*. He don't have to have a whole pocketful of plastic. The man'll come out there to stop you and he'll want to check everything you've got, and it'll take you half an hour to find it, going through all the cards you've got. You get to a card and, "No, this ain't the right one."

Historically, piling laws onto people engaged in activities that interfere with the plans of the powerful has been effective in clearing away that pesky free-market mechanism we call competition. In Puerto Rico, following the takeover of the island by the Americans, around the turn of the century, mainland businessmen required that several home-based, small-scale enterprises that produced food and drug products be pushed aside to make room for larger food and drug manufacturers backed by mainland capital. Cigar manufacturing, liquor distilling, and household milk production—all small-scale pursuits that families undertook to make ends meet—were outlawed shortly after the United States assumed control of the island, primarily on the grounds that they threatened public health. Outlawing small-business activities like these results, predictably, in clearing the market for big manufacturers who can produce liquor, cigars, and milk in facilities the government approves as clean. Often, of course, large manufacturers are partially responsible for setting standards that smaller producers have difficulty adhering to, only to object to the rigidity of such standards once the smaller producers have been run out of business.

What happens to the people who once fleshed out spare household incomes by making and selling milk, liquor, and cigars? How they behave is less predictable. Some move into alternative small businesses that require little capital investment and are not, yet, against the law. Others begin working for someone else, often for the very interests that drove them out of business in the first place. Still others continue producing, but in a clandestine way, entering underground economies and peddling their wares on the black market.

Whenever people trying to make ends meet become outlaws for the ways they make ends meet, they begin questioning those who made them outlaws. I once asked Carl Garner, a Down East shrimp fisherman, how he kept his sense of humor after all the regulations pushed him into smaller and smaller fishing territories. He replied, "If we didn't have our senses of humor, we'd be like those guys who walk into the Post Office with automatic weapons and mow everybody down."

Carl was joking, but he was not far off. If people prevented from making a living by too many regulations and laws have no political power, they can easily become frustrated enough to lash out senselessly. Even as I write this, a North Carolina group calling themselves the "Freemen"—consisting primarily of part-time commercial fishermen—have been attending public hearings in order to proclaim their active resistance to new regulations on fishing imposed by the state, but at times they sound as threatening as the militia who surfaced throughout the United States after the Oklahoma City bombing. And if commercial fishers do not resort to shooting people, they *are* likely to turn their frustration inward and blame themselves, which in turn can lead to drinking to excess and other self-destructive behaviors.

Anthropologist Katherine Newman, after interviewing several insurance executives laid off during the 1980s, wrote:

> Downwardly mobile managers are left hanging and socially isolated with no stable sense of who they are. Trained to see identity as a matter of occupation, yet unable to claim a place in the business culture they came from, they remain socially disabled and

suspended in time. . . . They feel older than their years. Their
deviant career path throws into high relief the contrast between
younger, successful years and this middle-aged experience of failure and frustration. . . . The rest of the world seems to define them
as finished, old, washed up. After many years of fruitless attempts
to recapture a rightful place in American society, they often come
to see themselves in the same way.

Commercial fishers may internalize the difficulties that come from
government regulations, or lash out in the form of low-level militias like
the Freemen, blatantly ignoring or breaking new laws. Yet even if these
regulations are born of pressures from organizations or individuals interested in protecting the environment and conserving fishery resources,
pushing commercial fishers off the water, ironically, threatens the health
of estuaries and marine resources. Criminalizing Mid-Atlantic coastal
commercial fishing achieves exactly the opposite result desired by fishery regulators and by many of those who belong to recreational fishing
clubs or organizations dedicated to preserving the coast's beauty and
resources. As with the striped bass restrictions, many regulations restricting commercial fishing, while claiming to protect the resource, often
remove key players from the chain of predator-prey relationships.

Many who prey on the coast's resources, such as corporate hog farmers, phosphate miners, and pulp and paper manufacturers, would like
nothing better than to see commercial fishers disappear. Because fishers
move from one territory to another to fish, shift from crab pots to shrimp
trawls or from gill nets to clam rakes, because they land croaker during
one season and mullet or blue crabs during another, they are the group
of people best situated to monitor the health of coastal rivers, sounds,
ocean waters, and estuaries. They routinely spot and report incidents of
pollution. They experience the waters, often taking note of changes that
are too subtle and requiring too many observations for anyone but fishers to notice. They tickle the bottom with crab pots, assess the conditions of sea grasses snarled in their nets, witness in the debris of their
catch the litter of tourists and the natural trends in biological diversity.

How can recreational fishers or even part-time commercial fishers, coming and going irregularly, concentrating their efforts on weekends and during the summer months—how can they achieve the levels of observation that commercial fishers currently achieve day in and day out, throughout the year, all over the estuary? Without fishers on the water, what will stop the phosphate miners and forestry concerns from releasing the biohazards into the water and air when no one is looking? If fishers leave or are forced from the resource, who will assume the critical role of monitoring the waters with the expertise of the men and women born into fishing families? What marine biologist, volunteer citizen monitor, or Division of Marine Fisheries enforcement officer will work from 4 o'clock in the morning until nightfall in the same territory, feeling the bottom with his traps or his vessel's keel?

Most important, who can ever take the place of men like Carl Murphy, the Stumpy Point fisher who said, "Well, I've been fishing since I was a boy. I started when I was about thirteen on a shrimp boat. And I've fished every summer till I got out of high school. And I fished after then, until I went through college for a couple of years. Then I went in the Navy for four. I've been fishing ever since. I've fished all my life; I'm sixty-three years old. I can't hardly remember when I wasn't fishing. I'm as much a part of this sound as the things that live in it."

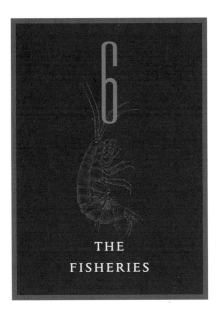

THE
FISHERIES

If many commercial fishers of the Mid-Atlantic Coast challenge simple description, they defy classification. Engaging in some of the most complex fishing strategies along the Atlantic Coast, one way commercial fishers deal with restrictions coming from recreational and development interests is to take up new gears, move into new waters, and take advantage of other fisheries. This is the way, historically, North Carolina watermen have adapted to natural fluctuations in fish stocks: by shifting among species, gears, and territories. Focusing on their behaviors in detail will provide a window into the practices of small and medium-size fishing operations up and down the Mid-Atlantic Coast. These behaviors make it difficult to pigeonhole many Mid-Atlantic fishers into designations according to the gears they use or the species they pursue and harvest.

This is unlike images of fishers in many other parts of the world. Anyone who has been to the coastal villages of Maine or Alaska, for example, has a pretty good idea of what a lobsterman or salmon fisherman looks like, and the pots or nets they use, the vessels they commandeer over the waves, the markets their catches supply. Yet in North Carolina, a man you at first think is a crabber, because he pulls and shakes crabs from 300 hundred pots into a 30-foot skiff in the Pamlico River, might also set gill nets for flounder or trawl for shrimp using other boats that he launches from other locations. Most likely he sets a bait net of some kind. His family may or may not operate a soft-shell crab peeler operation, lease clam beds, or rake oysters during the winter. North Carolina's geography and estuarine system encourage multiple fishery fishing, especially when boats are small enough to pull behind pickup trucks and launch from one of dozens of natural and manmade locations around the state.

Brief descriptions of the regional clusters of fishing practices in the state can help us better appreciate how comprehensively North Carolina's commercial fishers cover the coastal plain, watching, witnessing, paying attention. From Currituck Sound in the north to Calabash in the south, and from Hatteras Point in the east to where the Tar River becomes the Pamlico in the west, North Carolina fishers, daily, throughout the year, assess the condition of the waters and the surrounding landscapes of wetlands, marshes, submerged stretches of vegetation, and dunes.

Three primary peninsulas—between Albemarle Sound and the Pamlico River, between the Pamlico and Neuse Rivers, and the long strip of land we call Down East—along with the series of barrier islands separating the Atlantic from the coast, allow a high degree of movement among river, sound, and ocean and even among different fisheries. It is not uncommon for fishers living on any one of these peninsulas or barrier islands to fish in several locations in the surrounding waters, gaining access to them by hauling their vessels overland and launching them from one of many ramps or creeks, or mooring two or more vessels in different locations. During a recent study that collected information on North Carolina crabbing territories, for example, we found crabbers who set pots in the Alligator River early in the season, crossing over to

Fish market, New Bern, North Carolina, c. 1905

the Pungo during the early summer, and then fishing in the Pamlico River later in the summer. While North Carolina's complex coastal geography—dented and pierced with inlets, bays, and rivers—allows a great deal of flexibility, fishers' attachments to the marine ecosystem vary from place to place along several lines. The availability of fish and shellfish, the depth and salinity of the water, the jurisdictions of federal and state agencies, and the proximity to urban and tourist areas are only a few of the factors contributing to differences within the state's fisheries.

Five regional clusters of fishing practices emerge as we move from north to south and from east to west across the coastal plain: the southern region, including the Intracoastal Waterway and Atlantic waters from around Bogue Inlet to Calabash, near the South Carolina border; Carteret, or the waters around Down East and Bogue Banks; the Pamlico region, encompassing the waters of the Neuse and Pamlico Rivers and the people living along the western shores of the Pamlico Sound; the

Drying nets in Beaufort, North Carolina, c. 1900

Albemarle, Billy Gray's territory, stretching from Plymouth to the Pamlico Sound; and the eastern region, including fishing families living along the Outer Banks and Wanchese. As we encounter fishers in these five regions, we observe differences in the fish and shellfish they catch, the vessels they pilot, the gears they use, and the difficulties they face as they try to make a living from the sea. Not every fisher in the state suffers from the abundance of striped bass that plagues Billy Gray, just as the creep of recreational fishing interests into commercially valuable waters proceeds more slowly and with fewer political problems in some regions than in others.

In a very broad sense, the regions are based on ecology. As in the prehistoric period, the Neuse River still serves as a rough boundary between the more complex fishing lifestyles in the northern part of the state and the somewhat simpler, more specialized fleets of shrimpers and oystermen of the southern region. It is not surprising that four of the five regional clusters of fishing lifestyles occur north of the Neuse.

That the Neuse, this centuries-old border between north and south, should be so threatened by nutrient-loading from municipal sewage, forestry, and agriculture is itself a dark commentary on how much most of us ignore significant natural signals. In a group discussion I arranged with fishermen and fishermen's wives in Beaufort, Bryant Neil commented, "The reason there's no croakers in the Neuse River is that he come through Drum Inlet and swam around Pointy Marsh and started up the Neuse River and he puked and had to go back in the ocean."

The graphic nature of this observation reflects the depth of fishers' concern over the health of this ancient dividing line. Because the Neuse empties into the Pamlico Sound, bending north along the western edge of Down East, fishers from several regions of the state have a stake in its welfare. Its polluted condition not only drives fish back into smaller and smaller spaces, it increases the river's significance as a divide. The river begins north of the Raleigh–Durham–Chapel Hill triangle, winding through the metropolitan area and on through Goldsboro, Kinston, and New Bern before bending north and spilling whatever waste it gathered along the way into the Pamlico Sound. At New Bern the Neuse's status as a north-south boundary becomes confused with other natural features. South of New Bern it runs along the northern edge of the Croatan National Forest, a broad stand of piney woods that serves as a coastal buffer between the Neuse and White Oak Rivers. The White Oak separates Carteret and Onslow Counties and joins Bogue Inlet. The fisheries and fish-processing facilities that are centered around blue crabs become less common south of Bogue Inlet, taking a back seat to the shrimping and flounder-fishing traditions that line the Intracoastal Waterway and the mouths of rivers that empty into the Atlantic around Cape Fear.

The rivers of the southern region carry a lion's share of the region's hog and turkey excrement, coursing through counties like Sampson and Duplin, the former the county with the most hogs in the United States, the latter boasting the largest turkey-processing plant in the world and the headquarters of one of the nation's largest hog empires, the founding father of corporate hog production. Decades of draining the runoffs of hog and turkey farms have contributed to the devastation of the oyster gardens of the southern region, once a prosperous fishery that supported part-time and full-time fishing operations as well as a handful of vibrant shucking operations. Once these oyster gardens supplied raw bars from Wilmington to Myrtle Beach and seafood dealers with connections all along the eastern seaboard. In the mid-1980s, oyster-shucking houses in Wilmington, Shallotte Point, and Grissetown employed more than 100 workers in every month that, the saying goes, contained the letter "r." Ten years later, by the time I was interviewing fishers in the area for a governor's committee, the industry was dead.

Frank and Mabel Lewis, an elderly couple from Holly Ridge, oystered for several years, Mabel since she was a child, working with her father, and Frank since he retired from the military. "I was raised on the oyster lot," Mabel said. "Born on the oyster lot and raised on one, I reckon. We'd farm in the summertime and oyster in the winter."

Over the years, Mabel and Frank have witnessed their oyster gardens deteriorate and more of their income go into lease payments to the state. Every year, they say, they lose more oysters to local thieves and find it ever more difficult to reseed the beds with shell. Frank sees this difficulty coming from a source that troubles many fishers in the southern region. "Well," he said, "I think man-made causes have caused more damage than anything else. Digging channels and canals and things like that in the waters and through the marshes. You can't do it now, but at one time they did. . . . So that got quite a few of the little bays and creeks and places like this, you know. I reckon one of the biggest things is all these boats going through our waterways, and when they're going through so fast and they're just throwing the water in waves and you hear it slap across the bays and creeks, it's throwing some of the bottom up."

Only by dredging and channeling water can many of the real-estate developments of the southern region continue to remain viable. At the

Oystering, Washington, North Carolina, c. 1884

heart of this development is the Wilmington metropolitan area, with its budding film industry and rapid population growth—one of the fastest-growing regions in the United States. Its residents spill over onto the barrier islands of Wrightsville Beach, Topsail Beach, Surf City, Sunset Beach, and Calabash. During the summer of 1996, Hurricanes Bertha and Fran, coming within weeks of one another, revealed how fragile the matchstick beach houses were and how unstable the islands themselves are. Parts of this string of islands are so unstable that federal agencies refuse to offer emergency assistance, and insurance companies refuse coverage to the people who, foolishly, continue to build.

It is behind these islands, in sheltered areas around Lockwoods Folly River, Shallotte Point, and along the Intracoastal Waterway, that the region's commercial fishing fleet keeps its vessels. The largest of the vessels here belong to shrimpers. Many have been built by local crafts-

Oyster planting, Broad Creek, North Carolina, c. 1935

men. A short book by Richard and Barbara Kelly entitled *The Carolina Watermen: Bug Hunters and Boatbuilders,* lists 43 vessels built by Billy Varnum from 1966 to 1991, ranging in size from 35 to 96 feet in length and 12 to 25 feet across. These vessels have changed little in design, but quite substantially in their rigging, size, and power over the past fifty to sixty years.

They are, to my thinking, the loveliest of fishing vessels, whether at rest or working the shrimp grounds. When at rest, the two nets hang like curtains from high outriggers, leaning to the starboard and port sides behind the pilothouse. Approaching shrimping grounds, these net boughs come down and the nets flare out, giving the vessel a winged appearance; in the water, the nets open with the aid of two wooden doors and trail behind the boat like two long funnels. Near the ends of each net are the infamous "turtle excluder devices," also known euphemistically as "trawler efficiency devices" and, more commonly, simply as TEDs. These are cube-shaped steel insets that open at the top to release sea turtles that would otherwise drown in the net. Under ideal conditions, they open only when turtles push against them, but most shrimpers agree that it's like having a hole the size of a turtle near the end of your net.

Shrimping is primarily a summer fishery, and shrimpers of the southern region deal with the seasonal fluctuations in shrimp populations in two ways: by migrating into South Carolina later in the season, and, like other North Carolina fishers, by moving into other fisheries, particularly croaker, flounder, and other finfish. Many shrimpers switch to harvesting finfish and clams during the winter months, using smaller boats and clam rakes and gill nets instead of the otter trawls they pull for shrimp.

The mix of finfishing, clamming, oystering, and shrimping in the southern region takes place in a setting that is becoming increasingly dominated by the urban pull of Wilmington. Situated about midway between the South Carolina border and Bogue Inlet, Wilmington dominates the southern region, and the recent growth and economic diversification of Wilmington and New Hanover County accounts for many of the nearby commercial fishing practices. The proximity of a variety of jobs in Wilmington means that many fishers in this region move not only between fisheries as the seasons change, but also between fishing and shore-based jobs. This strategy has accompanied urban growth elsewhere in the state. In Carteret County the early-morning traffic from Down East communities like Davis, Atlantic, and Marshallburg to the Marine Air Base at Cherry Point thickens with part-time commercial fishers. Barbara Garrity-Blake, an anthropologist who has produced the best work to date on the North Carolina menhaden industry, studied part-time fishers in Carteret County and found that some of them have combined fishing and onshore jobs for many years. In the southern region too it is especially common for oyster fishers and clammers to leave fishing for months or even years at a time, returning to the water whenever they can. Spending even one season seriously doing commercial fishing, it seems, takes hold of one's desires for life.

The Carteret region and the southern region share other features as well. The combination of shrimping during the summer months, and finfishing and shellfishing for clams, oysters, and scallops during the winter, also encourages operating different vessels and using different gears. Along with the Nags Head / Kill Devil Hills tourist mecca to the north, Beaufort, Morehead City, and Bogue Banks of Carteret are as popular for tourists as the Wilmington area. It may be that this kind of growth is intimately linked to the movement between fishing and alternative employments. As the tourist industry grows, it both creates jobs outside of fishing and infringes on the space of commercial fishing, pushing communities of fishers into small areas surrounded by beach houses and condominiums. It pushes and pulls, increasing land values and taxes and causing access and space conflicts while holding out the hope of a steady wage and more predictable, if often substandard, income.

Nobody knows this better than the people of Salter Path, on Bogue Banks, in the Carteret region. During the mid-1980s, I met a scallop fisher named Davis Evans as he opened scallops at a seafood house owned by relatives of his. He stood before a pile of live, gasping scallops at a small wooden cubicle inside the shucking house. He was a big man—not tall but stout, bearded, with bright red hair and red cheeks. His pretty blonde wife was with him, helping him shuck scallops. Unlike the blue-crab industry, which hires locals and now imports Mexican women, scallop-processing depends on the labor of fishing households. Catching scallops requires somewhat less expertise (though at times more exertion) than, say, catching shrimp, because the scallop beds are as well-known as the oyster and clam beds, but coordinating a commercial catch of scallops requires far more planning and community support than simply locating and raking up the scallops. The principal factor limiting the amount of scallops you can sell is not the catching of them but the opening or shucking of them. Anyone, of course, can open a few dozen scallops for themselves, but fifty bushels, twice a week, through the eight to twelve weeks of the season?

Women in scallopers' households and extended families know their importance in removing the delicate white meats from the shells. When I met Davis, his wife and mother-in-law were opening most of the scallops that he and his father-in-law had caught the day before. Other women occupied other little wooden spaces in the shucking house, also opening their husbands' and sons' and nephews' scallops. I asked a young girl of fifteen or sixteen how she happened to be doing this work and she said, "I'm just helpin' Daddy," and the owner of the shucking house said, "You might have noticed that each little booth represents a different fishing family and boat."

In the mid-1980s, interested in why scallop-shucking was accomplished by kinfolk while blue-crab and oyster factories relied on unrelated hired women, I made a few statistical calculations that suggested that the difference could be traced to the length of the season. The blue-crab and oyster seasons last months longer than the three to four months of the scallop season. Hiring workers for only three or four months a year, every year, to perform relatively unpleasant tasks, is a difficult thing to do. You can't simply count on the labor market. Farmers who produce perishable crops and need large numbers of workers to work for only a few weeks or months a year depend on a large and complex system of labor contractors, and these contractors depend on the nation's most vulnerable groups of people—new immigrants, refugees, illegal immigrants, minorities, drug addicts, winos, children, and so on—whom they recruit with methods that range from smuggling them across the border to enticing them into their crews with crack cocaine and over-proof wine.

Scallopers, bless them, have not resorted to such methods, relying instead on women in their families and occasional other relatives and friends, and taking advantage of the fact that, during the winter, in Salter Path, there are few other jobs for many of these individuals. If the season were to last into May, counting on these loving daughters and wives would be more difficult. Like many fishing families of the southern region, fishing families in Carteret often supplement fishing incomes with work outside of fishing. Even Davis, a scalloper from December to April and a shrimper during the summer months, for part of the year hires onto a large, factory-like scallop vessel as a crewman and works the scallop beds farther south.

I helped him scallop one cold December morning, boarding his skiff at 7 o'clock in the morning and journeying out to the scallop beds around Harker's Island. Davis warmed the insides of his gloves on his diesel exhaust pipes. His father-in-law, his crew, was with us—a quiet, efficient man much smaller than Davis. Davis himself smiled and laughed at every opportunity, enjoying the company of other fishers working the beds and having someone aboard whose ignorance of the sea he could use as a foil for harmless practical jokes.

This was Down East territory, home of the distinctive Tidewater English accent and some of the oldest fishing families in the United States. Davis, from nearby Bogue Banks, was one of those fishermen who stored his boat in one location during the winter, to glide back and forth over the scallop beds, and in another location during the summer, closer to home, to shrimp. Already that morning, several small boats coursed back and forth over the scallops, two-man crews dragging triangular nets through fields of these passive bivalves.

The actual harvest consists of lowering the net on a thick metal triangular frame, dragging it along the bottom for a few minutes, then hoisting the full net by hand into the back of the skiff, emptying its contents, and returning it to the water. During subsequent drags, Davis and his father-in-law sorted through the catch, separating the scallops from the other debris and measuring the scallops into a plastic bushel basket before pouring them into burlap bags. They caught their limit, 50 bushels, in about four hours.

Though serious business, it was not done seriously. Davis hauled and sorted, piloted his skiff, and spoke and gestured in a convivial, jovial way. He joked to other scallopers in nearby boats that I was the revenue man. He toyed with the sea grass as you might tangle your fingers in a lover's hair, as much to draw her near as to feel her essence. Each time Davis pulled the net into his skiff, he examined its contents. More than once he showed me small organisms that resembled insect larvae and commented that they were more or less plentiful than they had been during past seasons. To me they all looked the same. He ate raw clams and asked me about small, translucent life forms that I would not have been able to tell from a Japanese noodle.

Davis was, in his jocular and carefree way, keeping a close watch on the sea. As a doting son might tease his mother and father for the stories they tell or the tidbits of packaged wisdom they repeat again and again—all the while listening, learning, believing—Davis played with the water and its offerings, joked about them and used them as his props, yet listened to them and watched them, noticing changes in their appearances and behaviors and growing concerned about new developments he did not understand. A loving child could express no more worry over the haphazard memory lapses of a parent with Alzheimer's than Davis would express when, only years after this short fishing excursion, an algae bloom choked the scallop grounds.

And who else but men like Davis are in a position to notice these changes, the signs leading up to algae blooms, the season-by-season fluctuations in fish stocks? Forced onto the shore to make ends meet with a job, fishers threaten that position, that intimacy. Full-time fishers see it happening all the time. They notice that fishers who leave fishing for a full-time job ashore, phasing back to part-time fishing, slowly lose the ability and perhaps the motivation to continue monitoring and protecting the resource. They simply cannot spend the time it takes to maintain the necessary level of attention and stewardship, a fact that is reflected in their tendency to shift to fishing methods that are less labor-intensive, such as nets or crab and fish pots.

In fact, they may begin to harm the estuary. Too often, full-time fishers complain, part-timers leave their gear in the water for too long, checking traps and nets only weekly instead of daily, and having to throw away the fish, crab, and eels that became entangled in the net or were entrapped and died in the first hours of soaking.

As Billy Gray's and Roly's comments suggest, fishers of the two inside regions, Pamlico and Albemarle, have the most trouble with part-time fishers. The primary gear in these regions are crab pots and stationary gill and pound nets; Albemarle fishers also set eel pots. Full-time fishers like Billy Gray fish these daily. From March or April until November or December, whenever a hurricane isn't brewing or the planets aren't aligned in a way that has an unfortunate meteorological effect, it is not uncommon to see crabbers in their wide, flat boats puttering along a string of floats, pulling pots and shaking crabs into tall plastic buckets the size of garbage cans.

The process itself is laborious, especially for fishers who do not use winches, but those who know what they are doing endow the process with a certain rhythmic timing. Pulling up to one of the floats, the experienced crabber reaches underneath with a hook attached to a long pole, pulls the line out of the water, grabs the line, and lifts the trap up and into the vessel, opening its top and letting the crabs scatter into the vessel, then baits the line and returns it to the water. The entire process takes less than a minute, but it may be repeated as many as 300 or 350 times a day, every day, six days a week, from around 5 o'clock in the morning until around 2 o'clock in the afternoon. Breaking the monotony is an early morning visit to the pound net for bait fish and a visit at the end of the day to the dealer's or processor's dock. Referring to this level of effort, a dark-haired, lean young crabber from the Pamlico region, Henry Decker, once told me, "A man pulls 300 a day by hisself six days a week, he's had enough."

Blue crabs lie at the heart of North Carolina's entire fishing industry, the main fishery of two of the state's five fishing regions—Pamlico and Albemarle—and are important to the fishers of Down East and the Outer Banks as well. Only in the southern region is crabbing relatively incidental to the other fisheries described earlier. The fishers in the Pamlico and Albemarle regions are the premier crabbers in the state, sometimes setting as many as 600 or 700 crab pots through the year.

Pots are a stationary gear only while they are fishing, but crabbers move their pots through the season as the crabs migrate across the estuary, and when it becomes illegal to block certain channels to navigation with lines of floats and pots. Another reason crabbers might move their traps is to avoid "dead water"—water with so little oxygen that the crabs struggle to the tops of the traps in shallow water, trying to break the surface to breathe. Larry Elvers, a Pamlico crabber, once said: "Me, I got to where my water got in so bad shape, from June right on through September, the water's dead. I mean, you got to get up in two or three foot of water, because the crabs can't live out there in that. I mean, they might live out there, but if you pot them out there in that deep water and they can't move, there's no oxygen there and they die. . . . The water gets in such bad shape out here they start dying."

"When it gets so hot, yeah," Henry Decker agreed. "The only thing you can do is move your pots."

Whenever crabbers move their pots they run the risk of moving into another crabber's territory. Crabbers don't own the water any more than anyone else, but most of those who have worked the water for years respect another crabber's space once that other crabber has set traps. The rule of thumb is to stay 30 or more yards away from someone else's traps. This unspoken code of conduct has its limits, of course, and the conflicts between crabbers over the question of territory are tied to two main problems facing full-time crabbers of the Pamlico and Albemarle: first, crab processors sponsoring their own, large crabbing fleets, often with immigrant labor, and second, part-time crabbing.

These two developments are tied to blue-crab processor/dealers in key ways. What the processors are doing is an old, old story. They are expanding their capacity to produce, first by supplementing family labor with hired labor and then by replacing family methods of producing with typical factory production methods. In the Albemarle and Pamlico regions, this occurs on the water and in the processing plants, but more subtly on the water. While it is becoming more common among fishers in North Carolina to use their wives as crew—and it has always been common, as in farming, to use sons and sometimes daughters as crew— many fishing families hire or work with crew from outside the family. During the summer in particular, a man may hire a local high school student for either a daily or hourly wage, or two brothers may crab together and share the revenues from the catch, sometimes first paying the trip expenses or, as some fishers say, giving a share to the vessel. An ambitious crabber may put a son or an experienced crewman on a second vessel as a way of expanding his crabbing operation—again, much like a farmer might put a second man on a second cultivator—but rarely do true family fishing enterprises in North Carolina consist of more than two or three vessels.

The same has not been true of some crab processors in the Albemarle and Pamlico region, the same fellows who in recent years have been importing Mexican women. Their story, again, is an old one. Fishers in several parts of the world have always had somewhat difficult relations with dealers and processors who want to control not only the cleaning, shucking, and picking of fish and shellfish, but also the harvesting. When fish dealers and processors move into the harvesting sector, they often get in by means of formal and informal indebtedness. In its simplest manifestation, a processor loans money to crabbers on the condition that the crabbers sell the crabs they catch to the processor. Some, for example, encourage crabbers to land their crabs at their processing facilities by offering them loans to purchase or operate boats, perhaps buying or replacing damaged crab pots and floats. Others may give them a place to store and launch their vessels. Still others may cultivate paternalistic relations with crabbers, bailing them out of trouble or helping them in bad financial times.

There is something of the sense of gift-giving in these relationships, but it is the kind of gift-giving that some anthropologists call "negative reciprocity." How can reciprocity be negative? It is negative when the thing given is given with the expectation of receiving more than the original thing's value in the future. This is the antithesis of the gift: obligations created not for the maintenance of healthy, meaningful, and equivalent social relations but for creating and maintaining inequality. Processors engage in negative reciprocity whenever they attempt to make fishers indebted to their operations and thereby to rob them of their independence.

This practice is well known to those who are familiar with the history of fisheries, in North Carolina and elsewhere. Early European cod fisheries of the North Atlantic and Newfoundland were organized by merchants based in Europe, who outfitted men to spend months abroad in fish camps or on harsh islands or to establish small coastal settlements of fishers. Fishers in these places and times usually were dependent on merchants for gear, space on vessels or the vessels themselves, and in some cases supplies to see them through harsh northern winters. Merchants who became dissatisfied with particular fishers for one reason or another could cut off their access to gear, fishing grounds, and winter supplies. Such power, nearly as absolute as a monarch's under such conditions, does not breed good relations, and fishers who try to circumvent or resist the power of the seafood dealers and processors are often harshly punished.

Crabbers in the Pamlico and Albemarle regions know the consequences of these strained relations all too intimately. While crab processors and dealers have always tried to tie independent crabbers to their operations by advancing crabbers' trip expenses, providing them with storage space or sheltered docking facilities, and lending them money for gear or household expenses, these practices expanded and became more complex in recent years. Several developments encouraged this.

The influx of Mexican women was probably the precipitating factor. With a resident and highly pliable labor force, crab processors had incentives to keep the piles of steamed crabs in front of the women replenished as often as possible. Idle crab pickers constitute a lost opportunity and complain about lack of work (and pay) besides. Left idle too long, immigrant women are all the more likely to develop ties with other immigrant men in the area and—as they call becoming part of the country's illegal immigrant population—jump ship.

One processor in Pamlico County, an old fellow I'll call Gordon Smith, addressed the increased demand for blue crab after the arrival of the Mexican women by putting Mexican men on boats to set pots and supply his plant with crab. Initially, this was illegal. He began using male workers who had the same visas the Mexican women carried, not knowing or not remembering that those visas were issued only for people who entered the county for the sole purpose of working in crab processing. Crabbing—or harvesting crabs—is not an occupation that

Americans are unwilling to fill; many crabbers would insist that there are already too many people catching crabs in North Carolina waters. A lack of Americans willing to work in a specific occupation is the central condition of issuing an H-2 visa, so Smith's use of the Mexicans in this capacity was a violation of the terms under which these workers were allowed to enter the United States.

As soon as Smith realized his mistake he corrected it, but not before perceiving the value of using Mexican workers on the water. Although he could no longer use workers carrying H-2 visas, Smith could hire Mexicans with other types of visas or, ironically, even Mexicans residing in the United States illegally, as long as the latter showed him two pieces of identification and provided a social security number. The big loophole in U.S. immigration law is that employers, potentially subject to fines of up to $1,000 per illegal immigrant that he or she "knowingly hires," need not verify the authenticity of the I.D.'s immigrants present. I once heard a lawyer counsel a group of employers who regularly hired immigrants about verifying a worker's legal status. "If the ink's dry and the photo isn't upside down," he said, "you can accept it as identification. You aren't in the business of enforcing immigration law."

Neither was Gordon Smith, but his use of H-2 workers was too patently illegal. Pulling these workers off the water and putting them to work in the plants, Smith replaced them with Mexican workers who showed him appropriate identification. Around the same time, under similar pressures to provide crab for Mexican crab pickers in the processing plants, two crab processors in the Albemarle region entered into business partnerships with several Vietnamese fishers, financing their trips to provide their plants with crab. About this, a crabber from Pamlico said: "As far as one person hiring a bunch of people to go out there and fish that hadn't fished before, you know, it's a lot of immigrants now. They can't communicate. You can't talk to them, and they don't know the rules of the road, you might say, out there. And this man that spends a half a million dollars on putting in gear out there, it's just taking away from the people that's made their living from it, that their roots are here."

The use of Mexican and Vietnamese crabbers, while changing the languages and faces we now find in the blue-crab fishery, built on the old practices of binding independent crabbers to specific crab-picking houses. It is difficult to get crab processors to admit it, but most crabbers can relate one or two stories about seafood dealers and processors that illustrate how much crab processors would like to have as many crabbers as possible under their thumbs. These stories reveal, too, that most crabbers would like to remain independent of the picking houses.

It was in the spirit of independence that Warren McCallum pioneered a new market for the live blue crabs around the same time the Mexicans began entering the industry. I spoke with Warren's wife, Rachel, one afternoon in late March, before the crabbing season began heating up. Rachel is a short, pretty woman with red hair and a round, bright face, the mother of two boys, and, with Warren, a shrewd co-manager of the household's crab fishery. She runs the household peeler operation, working eighteen hours a day during the height of the season to provide Pamlico County seafood dealers with soft-shell crabs. She describes herself, during this time of year, as "brain dead half the time," and she exists in a kind of haze of blue crabs and meals through much of the summer, up at 4:30 in the morning to see Warren off to check his traps, and working well after he returns, seven to twelve hours later, with the new crabs in the peeler tanks.

It was Rachel who told me about Warren's role in expanding the market for blue crabs. Until recently, she claimed, the crab processors and seafood dealers had a virtual monopoly on the market, convincing crabbers that the market for North Carolina basket crabs—live crabs shipped into the urban markets around Baltimore—died every year by July 4, primarily due to an abundance of Chesapeake Bay crabs after that date. After July 4 the crabbers had to sell to the processors at the processors' prices, which Rachel alleged were the product of collusion and price-fixing. Suspecting this, Warren drove to Baltimore to check on the processors' market information and found that, in fact, the basket market for North Carolina crabs was just as robust after Independence Day as before. This knowledge was itself a kind of Independence Day for the crabbers, giving them an alternative market to processing plants, the one they had known for years.

"In the past three or four years," said a Pamlico County crabber in the spring of 1996, "this basket market has gotten bigger and bigger and bigger. And the demand for them means higher prices than what it's worth to pick them. To the individual crabber, it's worth more money for us to ship them north than it is to sell them to the crab houses to pick."

From the processors' point of view this was unfortunate timing, for it coincided with an increase in demand for crabs at the processing plants. As more full-time crabbers turned to the basket market, processing-plant owners stepped up their attempts to bind as many crabbers as possible to their operations. A few began organizing their own fleets, in some cases depending on fishers from Mexico and Vietnam to crew their vessels. Among the principal beneficiaries of these processors' efforts were part-time crabbers, who could crab before and after work, or on weekends, with the assistance of the processors. Martin Asbed, a full-time crabber from Hoboken, in Beaufort County, explained to me how this worked:

> There was some thirty odd crabbers at the crab house in South Creek. And out of those thirty some odd people, five of them were full-time fishers. The rest came from Texasgulf [now PCS Phosphate]. That seafood dealer set their boats up and put their bait in the boat for them, had it all ready for whenever they got off work, so all they had to do was get in it and go. And when the people got back to the dock, they didn't unload the crab or nothing. He did it. That's all he had to do.

The result of all these developments in the Pamlico and Albemarle regions has been an increase in crab pots and a seasonal scramble to set more of one's pots out earlier and earlier every year. Some have responded to these crowds of pots by damaging or stealing another crabber's gear. Others now carry guns on the water and threaten anyone who gets too close to their floats. Others appeal to the legislature or the courts. Yet still others continue to expand their operations, pushing into waters they have never fished, hiring people they can treat like serfs, forcing full-time family crabbers into spaces too small to feed a family, like Warren's and Rachel's, of four. The family fishers are the true casualties of the crowding, the women and men with lifetime ties to the resource and a generational stake in its health. Their response has been one of dejection, anger, disgust.

When talking about those who set far more traps than they can possibly fish by themselves, those who are bankrolling fleets on the water and setting ever more pots earlier and earlier every year, Rachel McCallum shakes her head and, as though referring to dogs around a bitch in heat, says, "All they're doing is marking territory."

While many of the crabbers of the Pamlico and Albemarle are marking territory, crabbers of the fifth, the final region, spend their days and weeks traversing territory, moving between state and federal waters and engaging in fishing practices that bring them face to face with the National Marine Fisheries Service and the regional councils as often as with North Carolina legislators and regulators. State waters extend only three miles off the coast. Beyond that the laws of the federal government apply over another 197 miles. Pitted against the open ocean, the fishers of the eastern region have a distinctive face, different from fishers elsewhere in the state and, in some places, a more industrial character. Some 200 families operate fairly large, 60- to 80-foot vessels out of Wanchese, the fleets landing their catches of grey trout, flounder, mullet, perch, spot, croaker, bluefish, and other finfish at a handful of seafood dealers in and around the big Seafood Industrial Park on Roanoke Island's southern end.

Garrison Keillor makes an interesting point about the towns of Wanchese and Manteo in his book about "blue highways." He says that while the Native American for whom Manteo was named was as obsequious toward the English as a governor's yes-man, the town of Wanchese's namesake was sly and resistant, even treacherous, when the

English tried to woo him with visits to England and trinkets. Today the two towns demonstrate radically different behaviors toward outsiders. Manteo greets, welcomes, and fawns over tourists, while Wanchese, still primarily a fishing community, turns a cold shoulder on the kind of coastal development that attracts outsiders.

The Seafood Industrial Park conveys this as readily as any working harbor along the eastern seaboard. Several ships line the bulkhead encircling the harbor, sporting orange and yellow long-liners' buoys and nets on spools, moored in place by ropes as thick as Polish sausages. Cluttering the broad, flat expanses of cement and gravel stretching inland from the bulkhead are lengths of cable, cylinders of welder's oxygen, nets stretched out in the sun, machine parts, and drums filled with lubricants. Men clad in yellow rubber aprons and white rubber boots perform the daily miracles of maintenance. Ice machines pepper the shore. Structures the size of tobacco warehouses rise irregularly along the water, and an adjoining field has become a graveyard of refrigerated trucks, the letters and happy anthropomorphized fish of their logos wearing away.

The park smells of fish and fuel. It recalls the industrial docks of Gloucester and New Bedford, Massachusetts, home for the largest fleets of industrial fishers on the Atlantic Shore. In fact, Wanchese, along with Norfolk, serves as a southern winter port for a portion of New England's ailing cod fleet. Some of the same fishers who off-load cod and haddock at New York's Fulton Fish Market, or at the auction in Portland, Maine, land monkfish livers, flounder, and grey trout in Wanchese. Like the industrial fleets of New England, too, many of the fisheries operating out of Wanchese use nets as their principal gear.

Gill nets, sink nets, and roller or trawl nets are the primary gear of the eastern region, distinct from the crab pot that anchors the fisheries of the Pamlico and Albemarle regions, the shrimp trawl at the core of the fisheries of the South, and the combination trawl and pot fisheries of Down East. The fishers of the eastern region probably share more characteristics with the fishers of Down East than with the others, emerging from whaling backgrounds similar to Beaufort and sharing with the big menhaden fleets an industrial character.

Yet fishers of Wanchese, the Outer Banks, and the other areas of the eastern region remain distinct from fisheries in other parts of the state. Along with their love of nets, fishers of this region fish far more heavily during the winter months than fishers elsewhere, intercepting schools of migrating fish as they move to their winter grounds off Hatteras from as far north as Newfoundland and Nova Scotia. Targeting species that move in from other, more distant waters influences many of the things fishers here have to say about fishing and fisheries. Responding to a question about the crowding together of nets in the waters off Ocracoke, Kevin Felding, a commercial fisherman for thirty-five years and the great-grandson, grandson, and son of fishermen, said:

> The only thing I see here on the space is going to be the flounder pound nets, and that's not coming from this area, people right here. That's coming from below us: it's Cedar Island people moving out of Core Sound and moving up here. There's so many nets in that area that so many people set so close together that they're cutting one another's throats. And people's bailing out of there and moving up here, because they think it's the people farther up on this end's catching the fish before they get to them.

Intercepting fish in the open ocean, fishers of this region may spend more time at sea than the day trips common among others in the state, prompting the inevitable adjustments of family, as Peggy Neiman, a fisherman's wife, suggests:

> When we first got married, he [her husband] was a commercial fisherman working on trawl boats, and they traveled up and down the coast, came in Wanchese mostly in the winter. They were floundering. Then it got where we had children and he was gone a lot and he wanted to be home. So he got off the trawl boats and worked here in the sounds. In the winter he oystered. In the spring he went long-netting, a little bit of crabbing in the summer—more

or less just playing with the crabbing, he didn't do a whole lot of that.

Fishers of the eastern region have this option. Like other fishers in the state, they move among gear types and target different species, crossing from one fishery to another through the year, but they have the additional advantage (and sometimes disadvantage) of moving relatively easily from one political jurisdiction to another. When the policies of the state government threaten them, they can move into federal waters, and when the policies of the feds irritate them they can cross over the three-mile line and fish, as they say, "inside." Similarly, shrimpers from the southern region cross into South Carolina to shrimp, and fishers from the Beaufort/Morehead areas sometimes venture out into federal territory, but fishers along the Outer Banks practice this most explicitly. There are disadvantages to this as well, of course: fishers in this region also need to learn two sets of regulations—state and federal—and deal with two sets of enforcement personnel.

Such strategic use of borders and political jurisdictions is common among groups that exist along borders and in some ways exist at the margins of society. I don't want to make it sound as though fishers of the eastern region are marginals, at least not in the same sense that people who, say, prowl through the streets at night, unemployed and unemployable, are marginals. Yet it should be clear by now that many of North Carolina's fishers aren't exactly at the core of the state's political and economic establishment, the heart of wealth and power. Quite freely, they have turned their backs on the formulas of politics and economics that would have them punch time clocks and submit to the crush of corporate hierarchies. In fact, one justification for allowing commercial fishers to continue fishing as they have for centuries—flexibly, moving among waters and species and gear—lies in the fact that they represent an alternative to most established ways of making a living, offering a critique, a commentary, on the distance most of us have placed between ourselves and the environment.

It is this sense that many commercial fishers are marginals, existing at the edges of other, more settled, more secure ways of life. Crossing from the jurisdiction of the state into the jurisdiction of the federal government and then crossing back, commercial fishers of the eastern region practice an age-old adaptation. In northern Iran and Iraq, groups of nomadic herders called the Yomut and the Komachi, since the founding of the early empires, moved east and west and north and south in response to political upheavals in Persia, the old Soviet Union, and, more recently, Azerbaijan, Iran, and Iraq. In the Kalahari Desert of the southern cone of Africa, the San peoples roamed across territories that traversed South Africa, Zimbabwe, and Angola, avoiding the cruelties of one government or other, ducking forced conscription for military service that has been a method that settled peoples commonly use for dealing with those they consider marginal. Closer to home, in southwestern North Carolina and northwestern South Carolina, moonshiners moved between the two states whenever law enforcement officers in one state nosed too closely around their stills.

Crossing from one set of laws to another allows the commercial fishers of the eastern region to dodge many of the assaults on the fishing way of life that have begun to enclose so many fishers of the state into boxes of inflexibility. David Stick, foremost popular historian of the Outer Banks, writes that the practice has not been confined simply to moving between state and federal waters. Many fishers of this region descend from long traditions of moving between different opportunities afforded by knowledge of the water. "The man who listed himself as a fisherman," Stick writes about the 1850s census, "might have been devoting an equal portion of his time to stock raising and hauling freight in his boat, while the boatman might have owned a net and done some fishing too."

Today this movement among water-based occupations includes a handful of skippers who operate charter boats for tourists during the summer, deploying sink nets through the winter. Perhaps because of their somewhat unique ability to migrate between jurisdictions, commercial fishers of the eastern region, when I spoke with them, seemed far less concerned about the state legislature's proposed assaults on commercial fishers than many of the others I spoke with elsewhere in the state. They are not, of course, completely complacent about developments in Raleigh, and one of the principal spokespeople for commercial fishers all over the state, Susan West, comes from Buxton, near Hatteras. Yet their fundamental fears point not to state legislators as much as to an ultimately more threatening foe, one whose influence is displacing their very lifestyles from the water, revising history, rewriting the biography of the coast.

7

REWRITING
THE
COAST

I'd shoveled coal and cinders,
Sand and dirt, even manure in my meager time, but nothing
That wanted to be somewhere else and something else so badly.
—David Wagoner, *My Father's Wall*

Just a block up the slope of the Cape Fear River valley in Wilmington,
North Carolina, the Cafe Phoenix attracts tourists hoping to glimpse a
celebrity working on a film at Carolco Studios. The gossips whisper
hopes of Dennis Hopper or Andy Griffith, but anyone will suffice—a
brother of Rob Lowe, a lesser-known Baldwin—anyone whose face has
been and will be again on a theater or television screen. Last summer,
walking along the Wilmington riverfront downstream from the obsolete
battleship, I watched three young models performing that hair-swishing
dance for photographers, making an ad for shampoo or skin cream,
doing their part to make the world a cleaner, more perfumed place.

Wilmington has become like that: clean, chic, where fantasy pushes ever more of the city's working harbor upriver or farther off shore.

So divorced from the working waterfront has Wilmington become that at the Café Phoenix most of the shrimp they serve over angel-hair pasta with pine nuts and sun-dried tomatoes come from overseas, even though less than 20 miles south, in Varnumtown, shrimpers land thousands of pounds of shrimp at fish houses along the Lockwood Folly River. The patrons of the Phoenix, renting beach houses or rooms at the Blockade Runner Hotel, may actually see the shrimpers in the distance—a few hundred yards off shore, working back and forth over the shrimp grounds—but they are not likely to see, up close, the industrial clutter of the docks, or smell the men who absorb the odors of the sea, or pass by the small frame houses and rusting trailers where fishing families live and weave their gill nets. Too much reality has a way of gumming up the fantasy of tourist and real-estate development along the nation's coasts.

Wilmington is not the only place this is happening. Nearly every inch of coastline, it seems, is up for grabs, for sale, a circumstance that cuts deep into the fishing way of life. I met with seven fishermen and three fishermen's wives in Beaufort on a January night in 1996, during the height of political debates and public hearings about new proposals to cloak North Carolina's coastal waters in an intricate layer of new laws. We talked about many of the suggested rule changes—closing clambeds, increasing licensing fees, limiting numbers of licenses issued—until slowly the talk coalesced around a single theme. Bryant Neil, a Down East fisherman who has spent more than forty years in and around North Carolina's waterways, introduced it by saying: "See, there's a deliberate conspiracy—you can believe it if you want to—to put fishermen out of the fishing business one minute, little bit at a time. If he can get you here, there, over yonder . . . when you lay down he's got you again. And that's what it is, little piece by piece by piece." Bryant went on to list some of the factors undermining his fishing practices over the past few years, mentioning regulations restricting shrimping to certain days of the week ("That's like telling a farmer he can't plant cabbage on

Thursdays") and the crowding that occurs when other fishers from other states come into North Carolina waters after fishing practices have been restricted elsewhere.

But that evening Bryant and the others had fewer problems with other commercial fishers from other states than with a potentially more devastating foe. Carl Mentloff, a shrimp and clam fisherman from Atlantic, said about a fisherman coming in from another state: "I don't blame him so much, because the man is trying to survive, he's trying to feed his kids. I can't get mad at him. I don't want him here, but I can't get mad at him."

"It would be the same thing," Alice Davis, a fisherman's wife from Harkers Island, said, "if it happened in North Carolina first."

"Right," Bryant agreed. "But he should have been able to stay where he was at and make a living. It's sad. What you're doing is attacking people on the lower rung of the economic ladder, and I don't understand that. That's what I don't understand. Now, if we were millionaires, I could see it."

At this point in the conversation one of the three women, Marcia Dews, the daughter, wife, and mother of fishermen from Down East who hadn't uttered more than seven or eight words all night, ventured to voice her opinion, saying softly at first: "It's political. One problem is these big investments. . . . If they could put commercial fishermen out of business, they can develop this whole blessed area."

When everyone chimed in their agreement all at once, and Carl boomed "That's it, right there!" Marcia felt good about going on. "I have a postcard at home. It was to him," she said, indicating her husband, "but I kept it. It said, 'Dear Mr. Dews . . .'"—Marcia paused to explain, "We bought some land Down East for $5,000 when we were children. We couldn't afford it now, but it's on a bay." Referring to postcard the again, she continued:

And it said, "We're looking for people with land the type of yours and we're very interested in closing quickly. If you're interested at all, please contact us at such-and-such toll-free number. We'll pay top dollar." The thing was postmarked, it was either Dallas or Houston, Texas. They had come down here and searched these court records and knew who owned anything that touched a piece of marsh or a piece of water. And we heard . . . that these Texas oilmen and big cattle ranchers out there wanted money to invest in developments and they had developed most of the Texas coast and they're after North Carolina.

"That's what's behind all of it," Alice said, "greed."

Marcia nodded and said, "So there's pressure on these politicians, and money behind these politicians, to get these people out of business. And it's like he [Byrant] said: They are nickel and diming 'em to death. While they're trying to fight one regulation, they heap on three over here. And the people down here are not doing it. The people in Raleigh are doing it, are getting it done."

Chipping away at the fishing way of life may or may not be a coordinated effort of a few powerful individuals, but it is occurring in a coordinated fashion nevertheless, with potentially grim consequences. There are, of course, changes taking place that create the image of political and economic conspiracy. The need for capital to expand, constantly, through investments in construction, drives the engine of coastal development, and in many cases there are no insidious or evil intentions behind the processes of growth that fishers so readily mark as conspiracy. Economic logic—and supporting ideologies of growth, efficiency, and productivity—are often far more responsible for undermining traditional ways of living than the motives of individuals are. Yet within these structures and political economic processes, relationships based on ethnic background, family, education, creditworthiness, and other indicators of social class result in the partnerships and justifications that the Bryant Neils and Carl Mentloffs of the world interpret as conspiracy.

When Marcia Dews said that Texas developers had completely developed the Texas coast and now were moving on to North Carolina's, she raised a point worth pursuing. What about these other states? What about other coastlines that have witnessed tourism and real-estate development go crazy? Closer to North Carolina than Texas is Florida, an East Coast destination for retirees and so-called snow birds for several decades, where coastal real-estate development is far advanced.

Over the past 100 years, most of coastal Florida has, in fact, been developed with an eye toward bringing in people from elsewhere, and one of the pioneers of this was a little known salt merchant turned railroad baron and development tycoon named Henry Flagler. Born in the Finger Lakes region of upstate New York in 1830, Flagler became a negotiator for Standard Oil, a business partner with the Rockefellers, and friend of the Vanderbilts, and in the last two decades of the nineteenth century he organized the building of a railroad into Key West, Florida. He was a tall, lanky man who in his twenties—photographed with a beard and top hat and carrying a shotgun—resembled the young woodsman Abe Lincoln. Like Lincoln too, Flagler married a woman named Mary, whom he institutionalized and divorced to marry a woman considerably younger. After his second wife went insane, he married a third in his later years.

One of several biographies of Flagler claims that he "took a frontier wilderness sparsely populated by scattered settlements of farmers, fishermen, and ship scavengers, and changed it into a twentieth-century superstate." Superstate? In 100 years, the superstate Flagler had a hand in creating suffers from a gloomy track record. While Disney and Anheuser-Busch expand fantasy worlds around Orlando and Tampa, other parts of the state foretell less delightful fortunes of places that hitch their fates to attracting droves of strangers and transients across their borders. An anthropologist at Florida International University, Alex Stepick, has co-edited two books about Miami that chronicle a city torn apart by more sporadic riots in recent history than any other, home to ethnic violence and drug-related killings, a metropolitan area that he and Alejandro Portes aptly refer to as "a city on the edge."

Florida's problems are not restricted to Miami. Many of Florida's retirement communities began as overglorified real-estate swindles financed by now failed savings-and-loan associations and designed to isolate unsuspecting elderly around overpriced convenience stores. Scattered throughout the state are failed condominium and marina developments, paved streets laid out in grids yet leading nowhere, and once-exclusive neighborhoods that have deteriorated into tenement housing, strings of prostitute motels, and ghettos.

During the early 1990s, conducting research on ethnic relations in Florida, I worked in a neighborhood like this called Northwood. Consisting of twenty or so blocks between Broadway and Dixie Highway around the border of West Palm Beach and Riviera Beach, in the 1930s and 1940s, Northwood was an exclusive tourist and retirement neighborhood. Pleasant motels rose and enclosed swimming pools and shared space with quaint stucco and white-frame houses, but by 1990 these had deteriorated into proletarian and immigrant roominghouses and the occasional homeless or domestic violence shelter. Less than five blocks away, the Intracoastal Waterway separated Northwood from Singer Island and other exclusive, wealthy barrier islands that stretch along the Atlantic Coast.

The island of Palm Beach was one of the first Atlantic Coast barrier island to adopt the path of keeping inland and waterfront neighborhoods separate from one another, physically, socially, culturally. In Florida this began with Flagler himself, who imported African-American and new immigrant workers from around the southern and eastern United States to build his railroad and his famous Royal Poinciana Hotel—in its day the largest wood structure in the world. During the hotel's construction, an African-American neighborhood emerged a few miles north of the hotel, connected to the hotel grounds by a series of footpaths. Named after a mythological Greek river that led to Hell, the Styx was a vibrant community of 400, alive with juke joints and shops that catered to ethnic tastes and styles. Even before Flagler colonized the island, Bahamian, Jamaican, and Haitian fishers moored their vessels at Palm Beach, and some stayed to provide the growing labor force with fish, to salvage shipwrecks, and to engage in transport and trade with vessels bringing supplies to Flagler's enterprises. As Flagler's hotel neared completion, Flagler established a tent city in West Palm Beach, across Lake Worth, and encouraged residents of the Styx to move. He wanted to use the prime real estate the Styx inhabited to build the Palm Beach Inn and today's exclusive country club known as the Breakers. Residents of the Styx refused to move, however, evidently preferring the coastal breezes and opportunities of water that the island offered over the mosquito-infested swamp cabbages of West Palm.

As Flagler's select guests began vacationing at the Royal Poinciana, as early as 1894, his desire to move the Styx increased, and by 1906 it was acute. Knowing that the British subjects on the island, the West Indians from Jamaica and the Bahamas, would be especially keyed up for Guy Fawkes Day, on November 5, 1906, the 300th anniversary of the conspirator's death, Flagler sponsored a circus across Lake Worth and provided free transportation to everyone from the Styx. While the people of the Styx were enjoying the clowns and acrobats, celebrating three centuries of the spirit of protest for liberation, Flagler's henchmen burned the Styx to the ground. No new African-American community ever rose from its ashes. Today the island of Palm Beach is so exclusively white that black and Latino service workers need passes to walk its streets at night, and it remains the only community in the United States with a pass law similar to South Africa's during apartheid.

Flagler's methods of ridding Palm Beach of any African-American presence may have been particularly ruthless, but time and time again the nation's coastal communities have been cleared of native populations to make way for exclusive use by the rich. On many of the sea islands of South Carolina and Georgia—most notably Hilton Head and Dau-fuskie—developers have all but destroyed the Gullah culture and African-American neighborhoods in their haste to build high-rise hotels, golf courses, and tennis courts. Ironically, such restricted-access developments almost inevitably depend on neighborhoods like the Styx or, today, like Northwood in West Palm Beach—that is, neighborhoods with cheap housing for people who work as chambermaids, dishwashers, busboys, and gardeners for minimum wage.

Walking through Northwood today, one would be hard-pressed to imagine the quaint tourist and retirement village of fifty years ago. The tourist motels have become prostitute lairs and labor camps for illegal immigrants and refugees. Harriet Mintz, a black woman who runs a funeral home in Northwood, said of the changes in her neighborhood:

> It was like one day this was a place where you could leave home and not have to lock your doors or, at worst, if you got in a fight at school, the worst that was gonna happen to you was you got scratched. . . . And all of a sudden it was just like, boom, crazy. One day you walked out your door and it was like, "You know, that neighborhood that they talk about on TV, this is here." And one day, actually, they were filming the bad areas of this area, and actually calling it a ghetto. We just laughed. We didn't know we lived in a ghetto, I mean, but our building was part of their little filming.

Around Harriet's building, hardworking Haitian refugees crowd into houses along the side streets, and Mayans arrive and depart in trucks belonging to landscaping crews, keeping the golf courses trim and clean. At the center of Northwood, a Baptist church feeds the homeless and refers domestic violence victims to the neighborhood spouse abuse shelter. Most of the restaurants, bookstores, the theater, the bowling alley, and the family-run grocery stores and dry cleaners closed long ago. The few businesses that replaced them or that linger on from the old days are those we normally associate with neighborhoods of the poor: pawn shops, check-cashing services, convenience stores thick with security measures. The Baptist minister lamented to me: "The white congregation of Northwood fled the community at the very time they should have stayed to deal with its problems." To cover the expenses of operating the soup kitchen, which feeds nearly 500 hungry and homeless every day, the church rents space in the building to Haitians for Catholic worship services.

Northwood is typical of neighborhoods within an hour's drive of exclusive resorts. Nearly every coastal strip of tourism has a neighborhood like Northwood, where its service and maintenance workers live, commuting to and from the resorts in public buses or labor contractors' vans, crossing the physical abyss between rich and poor. And it is not only the service employees who have been marginalized from these areas. Increasingly, working women and men throughout the economically diversified, working waterfronts of the coastal United States find themselves displaced by playgrounds for the rich and by copycat architecture going up around them. Among them, fishing families try ever more desperately to maintain their ways of life and keep tenuous holds over the coastal landscape.

The conspiracy that Bryant Neil claims is occurring along North Carolina's coast may not be as sinister as Flagler's conspiracy to burn down the Styx, or as well-coordinated as Bryant suspects, but coastal development there today is well on the way to creating a gap between rich and poor that is as sharp as the one that exists between Palm Beach and Northwood. It may not be as sinister or as coordinated, coming from capital's need to expand, but the coastal development is in many ways as underhanded, perverse, and deceptive as Flagler's sponsorship of a circus, celebrating an underdog's centuries-old protest while burning the homes of working families to the ground.

As in Flagler's case, the development occurring along much of the coast today results in restricting access to the fruits of sea and surf. More and more, only those who are wealthy enough to rent or buy property, or to keep up with rising property taxes, can enjoy the ocean breezes without stepping through the thick throngs of beachcombers. At nearly every public beach access point where parking is available, from Memorial Day to Labor Day a litter of loud music, umbrellas, beachtowels, and convenience-store Styrofoam daily develops around the steps leading to the parking lot. By contrast, along the miles and miles of beach where no parking is available, renters and owners of beachfront housing enjoy the calm of far lower densities of sunbathers and swimmers.

Municipal policies encourage this uneven peopling of the beach. Providing or restricting parking is one of the main ways that municipalities control the clumping up and unraveling of the crowds, but current trends in zoning threaten to widen the gap between public and private even more and further congest the stretches of sand and surf where people can park. In the words of an Emerald Isle city official, "If you develop a piece of property, you have to have one [beach access] every 500 feet dedicated to the public. Now, for the private subdivisions sometimes we waive that and go to the outer edge of their property so that we don't have public access going up to a private subdivision. And most of the time, we have required them to do a little something extra, more or less, make it twenty-five rather than a twelve-and-a-half-foot access on each side to compensate for losing one in the middle."

Similar schisms are occurring all across America. The rise in gated, secure communities—fantasy neighborhoods developed from the ground up and patrolled by private security forces—gives a solid, concrete, and authoritarian feel to the widening gap between rich and poor. Development along the nation's coasts reflects the increasing sense of insecurity in America, and the polarization of space that insecurity entails. Territorial disputes have become the centerpieces of land-use plans and zoning initiatives, civil wars mildly waged in the chambers of local governments and the cocktail parties of political campaigns.

Several years ago, at the end of a small conference of local fishery managers and interested academics, I attended a gathering of local politicians and coastal planners at the estate of a man running for the North Carolina state senate. People were already calling him "Senator," knowing his victory to be imminent, probably because the local political machine had picked as his opponent someone sure to lose. The senator's estate sat on one of the loveliest pieces of waterfront real estate I had ever seen, a small peninsula stretching into the sound, and the guests enjoyed blue crab cakes and cocktail shrimp and drinks served by beautiful young women. I tagged along to the party with a handful of my colleagues, but it was clear that the guests of honor were not the college professors, but the fishery managers from the conference, who were representing regional fishery management councils whose recommendations influenced fisheries policy from the Hudson River to the Florida Keys. Even before he assumed power, the senator knew well whom to flatter with free refreshments and pleasant talk for informal support in future fishery issues that link North Carolina to fisheries to the north and south. These fishery managers and the senator, who in fact later became one of North Carolina's most powerful statesmen, exchanged handshakes and business cards and parted on warm terms.

This was, of course, just good politics. But was it just? What makes me question the foundation of deal-making created in that setting of polo shirts and finery was a simple observation. Missing from the gathering were men like Carl Mentloff, Billy Gray, and Bryant Neil, weathered, leathery men who worked on the water, struggling with nets entangled in schools of striped bass and lamenting the piecemeal destruction of their way of life. It was not only that they weren't invited, for even if they had been, they would have had trouble dealing effectively with the senator and the fishery managers in a setting like this.

Gatherings like this expect and even require guests and hosts to follow myriad rules of conduct regarding eye contact, personal space, body language, tones of voice, and selection of words, phrases, even subjects. Most of these rules are unspoken, and many are so subtle that they register just below the surface of full consciousness. Infractions of these rules grate against goodwill without your realizing what it is that actually irritates you. They are cultural rules—rules learned by example, over the years, picked up from the company you keep through slow absorption of gestures and expressions into your own behavioral repertoire.

When fishers tell me that they feel out of place in settings like this, as out of place as they often feel at public hearings, I suspect that their lack of experience with the subtle cultural rules for these settings produces this sensation. French sociologist Pierre Bourdieu writes that these subtle rules of behavior and cues can help people create wealth, that they are forms of capital known as "cultural capital." Everyone possesses cultural capital, but the kind of cultural capital people possess varies from one social class to the next. A senator's store of cultural capital usually comes from years of listening to and participating in the glib oratories of statesmen, of attending country-club-like social functions, of lacing debates and speeches with touching anecdotes and cookie-cutter parables about tortoises and hares, blind men and elephants, tragedies of the commons.

The cultural capital of fishers, by contrast, is likely to run in another direction, in part because separating themselves culturally from people like the senator fosters a sense of group membership and pride, the feeling that their way of life is their own and not simply a poor imitation of another's. In this sense, the ways that Carl, Bryant, Marcia, and the others talk and act, the gestures they exchange, and their badges of clothes, mechanical expertise, knowledge of the bottom formations of estuaries and the habits of fish, constitute private property, but private property that cannot be bought or sold but only acquired through long association with other fishers.

It is property acquired, in short, as gifts are acquired, in the spirit of sharing, group membership, and cooperation.

The senator's cultural capital is no less private and inaccessible to people outside his social circles. To make a show of breaking through the barriers of cultural capital, people very much like the senator have created forums for open public debate of fishing regulations, inviting fishers from around the state to take part in their version of participatory democracy. Unfortunately these public hearings are based on the senator's ideas of space and discussion rather than those of fishers. When fishers debate an issue, they do so by methods and in settings that bear little resemblance to the classroom styles of public hearings. Nearly every time I encounter a gathering of fishers along the coast, it consists of a small group sitting together, usually in a circle or in a cluster that has no discernible structure, loose and flowing, with apparently no beginning and no end. These gatherings fray into radio conversations between vessels on the water and take shape again at the docks of fish houses and protected bays and harbors where fishers moor their boats.

The fluidity and spontaneity of fishers' gatherings make them somewhat difficult to locate and join, much less chronicle on video cameras, tape recorders, or with the equipment of stenographers and journalists. This is unfortunate, because it is inside public forums, so structured and scheduled, so accessible to the cameras and pens of journalists and the official scribes of the state, that the biography of the coast gets written and rewritten.

Anyone who has ever followed a public debate over a new law or a new development learns early on that these debates, hearings, testimonies, reports, and the like generate mountains of reading material. They leave a trail of documents that gradually coalesces into the official version of what transpired. Because so few of us are willing to sift through all that paper, all that formal "behooving" and "moving" and "yielding the floor," we rely on journalists and official spokespeople to boil the substance of these discussions down to what really happened: a kind of *Reader's Digest* account, reduced to literacy's lowest common denominator. In this digested form, these accounts penetrate the public consciousness, drowning out the voices of fishers that, without written or recorded texts, are lost to the coastal breezes or the atmospheric graveyards of radio waves.

The public debates and private parties of politicians constitute only a portion of the coastal property deals that take shape and reshape the history and geography of the coast largely beyond the reach of fishing families. Many of the legal, paper canals cutting into fishing ways of life pollute fishers' surroundings without ever involving those who have a stake in commercial fishing. Municipal and agricultural decisions to threaten water quality, coming from deep inside watersheds, rarely draw fishers or their family members into their debates. Even near the coast, some of the most destructive real-estate development takes place largely outside the circle of influence of fishing families. In the little town of Oriental, a Pamlico Sound community that has long been home to one of North Carolina's largest crabbing fleets, a dispute over the construction of a marina took place in a way that involved local crabbers only marginally, even though the original scope of the project would have further damaged an already contaminated nursery area.

The case began simply enough in September of 1989, when a development company applied for a permit to dredge out about nine acres of land for somewhere between 61 and 148 boat slips. The confusion about the number of slips should not be too surprising, for official and informal accounts of the business venture differ according to one's vested interest in or opposition to the marina. Confusion also exists regarding the position of the state. Some accounts say that the developers were given permits to build the marina freely, with no opposition from the state, while others insist that the developers slogged through whole swamps of red tape, hiring special scientific consultants, checking for shellfish populations, and satisfying rule after rule only to discover that yet another rule had not been followed.

My colleagues and I interviewed several individuals involved in the dispute. We were interested in the facts of the case, yet equally interested in how people for and against the marina perceived and represented those facts. Memory is highly selective, and exactly what and how much people remember influences what gets written down, whether it is written in court documents, newspaper accounts, or an anthropologist's field notes. Memory is, in short, one of the raw materials of history and biography.

First, the facts, as they have been established in courts of law. In late September 1989, Oriental Harbor Development Company Inc. applied for a dredge-and-fill permit to build a private marina in Smith Creek. Originally the company planned to build 148 boat slips taking up nearly six acres of water. They envisioned four floating docks—the shortest about the length of a football field, the longest about twice that, and all four of the docks eight feet wide. The complete marina would require excavating nine acres of wetlands.

Six months later, in March 1990, after consulting with North Carolina's Department of Administration, the Coastal Resources Commission issued the company the permit they requested. Here's where the trouble began. Two months after the permit was issued, several residents of Oriental, mostly coastal property owners themselves, including several members of the Oriental Yacht Club, contested the permit, claiming that building the marina would convert public lands into private property. The people opposing the marina drew on history, quoting previous judgments against private interests that wanted to rope off public lands for their own purposes. One ruling in particular came up again and again, a U.S. Supreme Court decision of 1892 regarding an attempt by the Illinois Central Railroad to privatize public lands, which reads, in its essential part: "The State can no more abdicate its trust over property in which the whole people are interested, like navigable waters and soils under them, so as to leave them entirely under the use and control of private parties, . . . than it can abdicate its police powers in the administration of government and the preservation of peace."

On the surface this seems straightforward enough. Granting the permit to Oriental Harbor Development was akin to exposing North Carolina's citizens to bandits by phasing out the police. But court cases are rarely cut and dried, and sure enough a little loophole in history opened a window of opportunity for the company. More-recent cases tinkered with the 1892 Supreme Court ruling and found that states could make their own determinations regarding which properties were in the public trust and which were not—that is, that states could in some cases allow privatization of public lands. Evidently, according to bureaucrats at the North Carolina Department of Administration and the Coastal Resources Commission, dredging out nine acres and putting in 148 boat slips, even though it threatened an already contaminated nursery area, was one such case.

Over the next two years, the yachtsmen and property owners of the town of Oriental contested the permit again and again, losing and appealing the verdict and finally winning in a limited fashion, succeeding in limiting the size of the marina but failing to stop construction altogether. Their lawyers argued the case based on the logic of the "public trust," citing the 1892 Supreme Court decision and clauses in North Carolina's constitution that outlined the state's responsibility with regard to waters and submerged lands that might benefit all the people. In addition, there was the concern that the marina might damage a primary nursery area, which enabled the yachtsmen and nearby property owners to garner support from local crabbers. Benny Waller, a crabber in Oriental for several years, summarized the crabbers' opposition to the marina when he said:

> I proposed the marina be closed; it wanted to go too big. Not because they wanted to put the marina there, but they just wanted

to take the whole area, and it was—it *is*—a very productive tributary, since the creek is closed as a primary nursery. I used to work up the creek and they say it's a primary nursery and you can't do anything. . . . The bottom of these creeks are silted, and if you don't turn that silt over and aerate it so that the gases and decomposition and so forth get out of there, it dies and becomes unproductive as far as a nursery area or anything else.

One of the men who stood to gain financially from the marina, Mickey Russo, countered this argument by first doing his own research and then hiring a scientific team, describing the process at length:

Well, I did some research as far as the history of shellfishing in the immediate area of this facility. Turned out, you could barely find an oyster if you spent your whole day looking for one. I presented this evidence to the Fisheries: "I understand you're objecting to this permit because you're afraid it's gonna impact shellfishing. But the fact of the matter is, there don't seem to be any." And their attitude was: "Well, we really don't care. We don't care if there are any shellfish there; it's the habitat we're protecting. If there were shellfish there, we want it to be in water clean enough to be harvested to eat raw."

Mickey expressed a narrow, disjointed understanding of the marine ecosystem. Ecologists know that when someone flushes a commode in Raleigh it affects the health of the entire Neuse River Basin, but Mickey, clouded by his investment, resisted believing that the stretch of creek he wanted to reconfigure was tied into a wider, dynamic ecosystem that supported not one or two shell fishermen but one of the largest crabbing fleets in the state. To help him resist and revise the state's definition of shellfish habitat, he hired a group of scientists, saying:

It cost $5,000 for this team to come for one day, and what they did is they spent half the day on the bottom in scuba gear, cataloging exactly what was in the creek. Their conclusion—they generated a very impressive document, which was their independent, objective, scientific evaluation of the waters—they found not one shellfish. And they did this with scuba gear and they were on the bottom. They weren't recreational, they weren't commercial shellfishers. They were scientists looking for shellfish. They couldn't find one. So they documented the fact that there weren't any shellfish; they documented some other facts that called into question whether this creek, which was also designated a primary nursery, was scientifically certifiable as a primary nursery. There was no evidence of that. This particular group says they put a lot of weight and value on submerged aquatic vegetation; they couldn't find any. What happens in some of these creeks is once you get off a sandy strip near shore, they turn into very soft silt, and through hundreds of years of siltation, the creek bottom is so soft that *anything* can't exist out there. Even sea grasses find it hard to find a place that's solid enough to stick a root into.

Like the arguments heard in court, Mickey's depended on history— the use of Smith Creek for shellfishing, the centuries of siltation—yet Mickey also forged an interpretation of Oriental's history that linked past and future, creating a vision for this sleepy little coastal village:

This whole part of the world, Pamlico County, this town of Oriental, flourished about forty or fifty years ago. There were automobile dealerships, there was a movie theater. I mean, this was a real economy at that time. There were sightseeing boats, there were party fishing boats coming in and out of the harbor. By twenty years ago, this had all ceased to exist. There used to be a railroad that came down here. This area had a heyday about fifty years ago and has been in decline ever since. So if you go back twenty years, well, there wasn't too much going on. It really wasn't. It was commercial fishermen fishing. The sailboat people hadn't discovered the area.

So if you want to go back fifty years, you come up with a different scenario than if you go back only twenty years. Boating was always a big activity, whether it was transportation of agricultural products or party fishing boats or sightseeing tours. There were boats on this river out here from here to New Bern—sightseeing boats. We don't have those anymore. . . . On the very same property that I was applying for this permit for, when the water goes down, you can see rails from where it was used to pull boats. There were marine railways, primarily for fishing boats. . . . So it wasn't that it was completely undiscovered until I happened onto the scene and wanted to put in a marina. There had been economic activity in the years past and that activity has declined. So it was really, for me, a task of regenerating some kind of economic activity, which this area sorely needs.

Pictures of Oriental entered the testimonies and narratives of most of those involved in the dispute, whether they were for or against. A member of the town's planning commission, Kevin Welsh, a recent refugee from the kind of development swallowing Morehead City and Beaufort, said:

What we're guided by is trying to make sure that what is done in Oriental, I'd say, preserves Oriental's uniqueness. And I love Oriental. I haven't been here long. I've known about it forever; I'm a native of Beaufort. And I would frankly not like to see happen to Oriental everything that's happened to Beaufort. Beaufort's held up as the great shining example, and in many ways it is, but there has been a tremendous amount of change to the Front Street of Beaufort. Real-estate values have soared and the population has changed. . . . Oriental has a true uniqueness in that it really hasn't changed radically. It's changed gradually and I think most of the changes have been for the good. I think if that marina goes in, . . . it needs to be scaled to suit the harbor.

Both Kevin and Mickey believed that historical continuity in Oriental's development, a smooth and logical link to the past, was valuable, yet the two men imagine and represent the town's history differently. Both men are attempting to characterize the cultural biography of Oriental in a way that allows them to add passages to that biography that have distinct yet concrete implications for future development. Mickey Russo envisions a bustling town of Oriental, a town of party boats and tourist motels, a town with renewed ties to New Bern and a boating heritage that, he claims, dried up between twenty and fifty years ago.

Kevin's is a vision of a sleepier town, a rural, pastoral Oriental, a place where people come to escape the kind of bustle that Mickey envisions. It is interesting that Andrew Peters, yet another investor in the disputed marina, characterized the marina in a way that was more in line with Kevin's vision than Mickey's, his own business partner. Peters said:

> It [the marina] would *enhance* what the use patterns are in this area; it wouldn't *create* a new use pattern. It would just enhance and support the existing businesses that are here. It would ensure the livelihoods of the people here that may be struggling because they don't have enough boats to work on or enough sails to make. It would ensure that their businesses would be successful and the tax base expansion would support the people that have retired here, that came here for several reasons: namely, low taxes, good quality of life. It would not affect the quality of life; in fact, it would enhance it by keeping the tax rate down. Oriental is a unique place. We don't derive our income from tourism. We derive our income from recreational boating and retirement. It's not a tourist area.

Recreational boating and retirement? Anyone who has ever been to Oriental knows that its waterfront is home to two of the largest blue-crab processing plants in the state. Several fishing vessels tie up between them, and a number of restaurants around the harbor depend heavily on local seafood. Yet in nearly all these facts and interpretations presented by men like Andrew, Kevin, and Mickey, in these versions of history and visions of future growth, in all this collective writing and revising of Oriental's cultural biography—in nearly everything of consequence about the marina and its size, location, effects on the environment—the local crabbing fleet and the larger processing and seafood industry enters only along the margins, drawn into the group opposing the marina on the grounds of environmental degradation.

But only someone who cannot see beneath surface explanations would believe that the dispute over the marina was ever really about public access or the contamination of the estuary. It was very much about Oriental's past and Oriental's future, but in ways that emphasize keeping access to the coast restricted to a wealthy few. Ironically, it was on the grounds of preserving the public trust that Oriental's yachtsmen and other property owners sought to keep their little stretch of coastline quiet and private, and it was on the grounds of expanding access to the public (the public that could afford to pay slip fees, anyway) that the company has been able to privatize as much of the coast as it has. Andrew Peters voiced all of this in an interview:

It has nothing to do with public trust or pollution or easements. The reason they [Oriental's yachtsmen and other property owners] don't want a marina built doesn't have anything to do with public access. The reason is they don't want any change. . . . One of the plaintiffs in this action made it known for many, many years through his local actions and his local statements to many people that he did not want the Oriental sewer system, he did not want the high-rise bridge, he does not want anything that constitutes change in Oriental. . . . He wants Oriental to stay the way it was at the turn of the century and never change. Now, what we're talking about is someone that doesn't want any progress or any change, yet the way they're fighting this project is they're bringing up issues of public trust, easements, environmental degradation, and everything else. But these are all just red herrings they're throwing up, because they don't want to see any change. It's very easy for someone who makes their living in Raleigh, who has substantial wealth and has acquired substantial wealth in the area of Raleigh, to come down here occasionally on the weekends and want to keep everything just like it is. But I think it's very self-serving and, unfortunately, its not in the best interests of the town of Oriental.

History is a kind of territory, a kind of property. I once asked a beggar on the streets of Washington, D.C., a man who asked for coins with an accent I could not place, where he was from, and he said, "If I knew where I was goin,' I might know where I was from." This street wit suggests a link between future and past that we see operating in Oriental and all along the southern coast. How we envision the future influences how we represent the past, and the visions of the future of North Carolina's coast held by Mickey Russo and Kevin Welsh are only two among several.

One of the most poorly informed visions I heard came from the Marine Fisheries Commission, when one of its commissioners suggested that the future of Mid-Atlantic Coast fisheries lay in the development of "boutique" or "designer" fisheries. This commissioner envisioned small and specialized fleets whose quaint facades inspired tourists to snap photographs and whose products appealed to coastal visitors the way gourmet coffees appeal to the languid shoppers of Manhattan and Seattle. It was a vision of the future of fisheries with little appreciation of the past. It was a clean, gift-shoppe version of the future of North Carolina fisheries, a fantasy, a vision of the kind that the poet Marvin Bell parodies in his poem "Gemwood":

> In the *shoppes*
> they're showing "gemwood":
> the buffed-up flakes of dye-fed pines—
> bright concentrics or bull's-eyes,
> wide-eyed on the rack of
> this newest "joint effort
> of man and nature."

If history is a kind of territory, a kind of property, as its importance in courts of law suggests, the idea of a town of Oriental oriented primarily toward the recreational boating and retirement set—like the idea of a clean and chic Wilmington or the revisionist vision of boutique fisheries—is a kind of theft, robbing the fishers of Oriental and the state of their past while paving over the artifacts of fishing that enable them to remember.

In a recent essay Lewis Hyde reminds us: "Every act of memory is also an act of forgetting." He is talking about the tendency to drown out the parts of our past that conflict with our sense of identity, that are mundane and everyday, or that are fraught with what he calls "wretchedness and anxiety." Immigrants at Ellis Island were encouraged to forget their roots to become Americans. For decades, African-Americans were not taught about the history of Frederick Douglas, Booker T. Washington, and W. E. B. Du Bois in public schools. Yankees moving west were encouraged to remember the glory days of the Spanish mission and to forget the commercial development of the East. Of this biased and damaged remembering Hyde writes:

> It was neither the missions nor their architecture that fed the Mission Revival. It was a novel, *Ramona,* by Helen Hunt Jackson, Emerson's favorite woman poet. Jackson's 1884 romance evoked a lost California paradise in which kindly Franciscan friars prayed quietly in their gardens, old Spanish dons dreamt their days away in cool adobe courtyards, and contented California Indians worked the fields, mission bells all the while ringing softly in the distance. Of the many available pasts (there *was,* after all, a Victorian railway depot in San Diego, not to mention a history of not-contented Native Americans), the world of the Spanish missions turned out to be the tradition of choice as the twentieth century began. It appealed strongly to transplanted Anglos, for one thing, who got to imagine that by entering a Franciscan past they were distancing themselves from the weary stress of Yankee commercial life.

One of the most influential books of the last twenty years has been anthropologist Eric Wolf's *Europe and the People Without History*, a chronicle of the past 500 years that sets down the raw materials of history for those of us from humble and modest bloodlines to remember. The people "without history"—the people who have been excluded from so many historical accounts and many of whose achievements occurred along the margins of official remembering—have been the working women and men of the kind who named Lake Mattamuskeet, who moved south out of Jamestown and settled the north coast of the Albemarle, who hunted whales from the barrier islands, who piloted vessels through the shallow waterways of the Chesapeake Bay and North Carolina's estuaries and into the wilds of the shifting shoals of the Atlantic.

These are some of the raw materials of memory for the working fishing families of the Mid-Atlantic. They rest on docks cluttered with crab traps and floats, they hang in tattered nets strung between pine trees for repair, they move along by means of diesel fuel, and they emit odors that offend and aromas that please. Remembering them involves envisioning the fishing lifestyle as a lifestyle intertwined with the estuary, an intimate component of the coast, a people who receive the estuary's gifts and give back the accumulated, rooted respect of knowing the coast.

VERSIONS
OF
HOME

In 1990 I met a man in the new citrus groves of southern Florida who was manager of a farm owned by a national fruit and vegetable company headquartered in California. We were outside a field office at the edge of newly cleared acreage, the white, sandy, smoldering landscape standing in sharp contrast to the green tangles of swamp that the company had not yet cleared. Neighboring this gutted and scarred landscape was the last remaining refuge of the North American panther. To the southeast, the Everglades choked from the seeping fertilizers of sugarcane fields and cattle ranches. Moving back and forth across the sand of the cleared space was an elephant of a vehicle, scraping the surface of the earth to a finish as smooth and white as the Bonneville Salt Flats. In the elephant's wake would come the engineers and hand laborers who would create a network of plastic pipe and plant young trees—rows and rows of two or three species of grapefruit and oranges that would forever displace the weedy, biodiverse tangles that once offered panthers sanctuary.

The man's name was Harold Williams. He was in his late forties and thickly built. His hands were rougher than mine, callused, and when we shook hands the muscles of his forearms participated in the greeting as though he was hoisting a bag of fertilizer. His job did not require manual labor—mostly he organized crews of workers with the labor contractors—so I wondered where his strength came from. We talked about changes in the citrus industry, especially its southern migration after freezes devastated the groves in central Florida.

This talk of devastation led to talk of crises facing farmers at other times and in other places, and it came out that Harold had owned his own farm, a family farm in Maryland, but that he had lost the farm early in the 1980s farm crisis and then struggled for a few years in the auto parts business before selling out and moving south. When I met him he had been a foreman for five years. Ironically, the agricultural firm that hired Harold flourished during the farm crisis, sending representatives into the distressed corn belts and breadbaskets of the Midwest to buy repossessed farm equipment at auctions for bargain prices, and negotiating with farmers in Maryland and Virginia to grow tomatoes for them during the summer months.

In more ways than one, Harold's loss was the fruit and vegetable firm's gain. They purchased farming equipment cheaply, negotiated sweet deals with the struggling Maryland farmers who had not yet lost their farms, and hired Harold from the ashes of foreclosure and dispossession, acquiring a farm manager with skills learned from half a lifetime spent on the farm.

Harold's move from family farming to dealing auto parts to becoming a farm manager was similar to the life transitions made by many men Harold's age and was in many ways the central American work experience of the twentieth century. In 1900, one out of every two to three people in the United States farmed for a living, yet by 1990 the proportion of the population engaged directly in agriculture had fallen to 3 percent, or about one out of every thirty people. One of the more powerful forces behind this change, the one most responsible for promoting the modern factory and the so-called advanced economic principles of production, was the auto industry. Assembly lines and other mass production techniques did not begin with the production of cars, trucks, tractors, and other vehicles based on internal combustion, but it was the automotive industry that first legitimized, then institutionalized, and finally rationalized the factory regimes of America.

Swept up in these economic tides, farmers like Harold Williams left their farms, but returned to agriculture under new conditions of ownership and tenancy. No longer an independent businessman, Harold had lost not only his independence but also his roots, his ties to the local region, the local ecosystem, and the local history into which he was born. By the time Harold returned to farming, now as somebody's employee rather than his own boss, Florida agriculture had been industrialized, and its influence was spreading out of Florida and into harvests up and down the eastern seaboard and into the corn belts and wheat belts of the American heartland.

For every new field, grove, and orchard that comes within the company's influence, the firm imposes its own standards of production, marketing arrangements, rules of employee conduct, and grounds for promotion, punishment, and dismissal. It replaces diverse crops and livestock and diverse farm-management styles with a narrower set of products and a single management regime. They import foreign labor for the harvests and ship everything the immigrant and refugee workers pick to distant markets, further chipping away at the sense that anybody or anything is local. In the wake of these altered production strategies, men like Harold Williams migrate first out of farming and subsequently out of their home regions altogether. Many who make these moves must leave behind houses that won't sell, schools with fewer and fewer students and tighter budgets, and municipal tax bases that shrink to levels where firemen, police, garbage collectors, and maintenance workers feel the pinch.

What does Harold's experience have to do with fishing? His life, his transition from farming to farm managing, from farm owner to farm employee, is a transition from relative independence to dependence that has occurred in many sectors of American life. It is a transition that is all too often accompanied by a loss of the social, cultural, and biological diversity on which life has always depended for responding to crisis and disaster. Fishers forced to leave fishing lose the independence and flexibility of movement that enable them to act as stewards of the resources. Passing through life phases similar to Harold's, first becoming part-time commercial fishers, their irregularly tended nets and pots may, in fact, damage the resources as they struggle to make ends meet with a diminished access to the estuary's gifts. They compromise the stewardship they knew as full-time fishers, reduce the number of species they target, limit their gear, and concentrate their fishing efforts in a way that seems unnatural and irrational to full-time fishers who continue to move among fishing territories, gear types, and fisheries through the year.

I suspect most of us have known someone like Harold Williams, someone disheartened by dispossession and stripped of independence. His experience and the experiences of others like him have touched and diminished the lives of nearly every American. We see the toll of these experiences in the faces of local merchants pushed out of business by Wal-Mart, of restaurant owners who cannot compete with the highly capitalized national chains, and of owners of the small, rambling motels forced out of business by Hilton and Marriott. We witness it in the middle manager laid off in the most recent wave of cutbacks, or in the formerly unionized worker whose once high-paying job has disappeared to an overseas producer and whose current, lower income derives from three part-time jobs without a pension plan or a health benefits package. More and more frequently, we hear its effect even on physicians and attorneys, forced out of private practice to work for the national HMOs and big corporate law firms.

Business managers and newspapers have euphemisms for it: restructuring, downsizing, streamlining. Yet such terms only convert into boardroom parlance the real experiences of people whose livelihoods have suffered from the corporate proposition—backed by laws and banks—that clearing aside small producers and small businessmen in the name of economic efficiency is a just enterprise. Along the Mid-Atlantic Coast this proposition takes the form of the tourist, leisure, and development interests that tacitly agree that the coast is more valuable as a source of pleasure than as a source of fish.

Never are the experiences of men like Harold strictly personal tragedies. They engage and involve entire families and communities by diminishing the store of expertise, knowledge, and memory that exists to cope with whatever crisis might arise or to prevent new crises from developing. They undermine the relationships that encourage and nurture meaningful exchanges of gifts between one another, and the exchanges of necessity and enjoyment that we make with our surroundings, our water, our land, our estuary. The changes taking place along the Mid-Atlantic Coast today threaten to dismantle those relationships as surely as the closing of factories, the downsizing of American corporations, and the spread of national chains has ripped apart communities and families in the wake of layoffs and factory closures.

Yet it may be those very community crises that show how shallow the allegiance of many national companies to anything local is. It may be these crises, drawing on the deep attachments that community members have to place, region, history, and ecosystem, that reveal the crucial strengths and weaknesses of the people being dispossessed, disenfranchised, and deprived of their ways of life. It may be these crises that teach us about how to prevent any more of the losses that we are witnessing today along the Mid-Atlantic Coast. It may be these crises, ultimately, that teach us that many commercial fishing families represent a stand against the creeping encroachment of a coast lined with high-rise hotels, a coast effectively closed to the public. Unchecked, that encroachment will first reduce social, cultural, and economic diversity along the coast, then move on to dispossess us of our coast and ruin our water quality as surely as closed-up factories leave behind nothing but unemployed people and carcinogenic stains.

Historically, attempts to prevent factory closings or to reinvigorate former centers of manufacturing have been feeble, and the efforts of Mid-

Atlantic commercial fishers to prevent the piecemeal destruction of their way of life are no exception. It has not been for lack of trying. If the fishing industry of the Mid-Atlantic Coast were a single body, we'd say its right hand didn't know what its left hand was doing.

Through this final decade of the twentieth century, several fishing organizations have formed to fight against the criminalization and destruction of the commercial fishing industry. They have waged sometimes quiet and sometimes loud battles against the federal and state legislatures, the Division of Marine Fisheries, the National Park Service, the National Marine Fisheries Service, and the organized arm of the recreational fishing industry now misnamed the Coastal Conservation Association. They have protested proposals to ban nets, to close seasons early, to modify equipment, and to restrict access to waters at certain locations or certain times. Some were formed by women, others by men; some were developed by those involved in shrimping, others by those who crab; some were organizations of processors and fishers, others only of one or the other; some recruited the aid of scientists, others spoke out against science; some sided with environmental groups, others had environmental groups speaking out against them; some flourished briefly, others lingered and linger still.

What they have in common besides all being somehow involved in commercial fishing and all being, somehow, sadly ineffective, is that they are all relatively local, tied to a narrow vision of region, a unique version of home. Mid-Atlantic fisheries are highly diverse and fragmented. Fishers in one community may know little about fishers living only fifty miles away. This is the case, currently, among fishers involved in a highly localized, yet symbolically important dispute taking place in eastern North Carolina among a small group of herring fishers on the Chowan River.

I'd like to end near where I began, in the herring fishery, working back through the investments of time, money, relationships, and heritage that forced Gabe Bishop to leave his pound nets along the Chowan River and to attempt to engage powerful people of the state in a kind of trade. In February 1996, Gabe drafted a letter to Bruce Freeman, then director of the North Carolina Division of Marine Fisheries, telling the director of his willingness and the willingness of neighboring fishers along the Chowan to reduce their pound nets by half. Together, these fishers called themselves the Chowan River Pound Net Fishermen, and their proposal stated in clear and polite terms that all the fishers who operated pound nets on the Chowan River, with one exception, had agreed to reduce their nets voluntarily.

There was no response. Gabe and his fellow fishers tried to contact people in the head office and in the regional office, but, Gabe recalled:

Last year I told Daddy—he was eighty years old—and I said, "I hope we have some fish on your birthday." His birthday was the third day of April, and the third day of April we caught 5,000 pounds of fish. It was a mild spring, the weather was a little bit milder, and we had a few fish, you know, like 3,000 or 4,000 pounds, there for two or three days. That was a little run of fish, and then they were gone. Well, the next week we had another little run of fish, and one day there I think we had 16,000 pounds. For about three days we caught up 10,000, 8,000 [pounds of herring].

Well, that run was gone on Wednesday. The season closed on Friday. Well, on Friday, the last day that we fished, I think the only thing we had was 400 or 500 pounds of fish. Well, the next Wednesday we went and fished—they told us we can fish *around* the herring, and put the herrings back. . . . Well, if you're not catching but 15 or 20, you can do that. But we told them you can't do it, that the fish were gonna come in, so no way in the world you could fish. They said, "You can," so we said okay. So instead of taking up [the nets]—we knew we weren't gonna be able to fish—we decided to leave the nets setting just to show them, and tried to get them down here, the Division down here, the biologists, and show them what was going on. Well, the next Wednesday a run of fish hit and we called them up, and could not get a soul in this world down here, nobody. Nobody wanted to come, didn't want to check the fish. Went to the top, . . . tried Bruce and everybody, tried to get them down here just to show them the amount of herrings that was out there and that you could not fish. No sirree! Could not get a soul. So we called the television station at Little Washington. They came down. We went out and pulled one net, and there was somewhere around 14,000 pounds of fish in that one net. 14,000 pounds! We pulled them up just to show them the amount of fish, and released them. . . . We went to nine nets that day and released about 60,000 pounds of fish, out of nine nets. I mean you cannot fish. We tried to tell them that.

When I questioned the biologists about this they said the fishers didn't understand about the dynamics of fish populations, particularly that several year-classes need to mature before the population was again viable. But Gabe has been a fisherman his entire life and comes from at least four generations of fishers before him. When you talk to him about water quality and fish populations, he demonstrates a detailed under-standing of a variety of factors affecting fish population levels, in addi-tion to overfishing. And like most Chowan River fishers, he places the pollutants from nearby pulp and paper mills, and various infrastructure developments that have made it more difficult for herring to swim as far as the Chowan, high on the list of dangers to fish.

However, despite all that Gabe Bishop and his fellow fishers may know about fish populations, the people at the Division of Marine Fish-eries were free not to listen. There are two reasons for this. First, they discounted the legitimacy of the fishers' complaints by appealing to fishery science, and, second, the high fragmentation of the fisheries of North Carolina made it possible for one group of fishers' complaints to be ignored even when fishers all over the state were complaining about the quality of fisheries management. The several small, grassroots orga-nizations of fishers that have levied complaints against fisheries manag-ers in the state have all been very local disputes, so tied to local historical circumstances that it has been relatively easy for fishery managers to ignore them.

Gabe believed that he was coming from a position of legitimacy and expertise, in part *because of* his personal role in the heritage of the fishery. Herring fishing in the waters we now call the Albemarle Sound and the Chowan and Roanoke Rivers predates European settlement of the region, and throughout the last three centuries, it has provided large numbers of seasonally abundant fish for fishing operations that range from small fisher farmers who salt herring as a critical source of protein through the year to large, highly capitalized fisheries that at one time hired hundreds of workers and today salt and pickle herring in wooden vats as large as the beds of pickup trucks.

Out of this tradition of a crucial seasonal subsistence and economic event, Gabe Bishop brought his complaint against the state, focusing the attention on fishers along a segment of North Carolina's coast. Perhaps he has not been successful because of the power of this local history, particularly its power to focus the Chowan fishers inward instead of outward toward establishing a broader base of power among fellow fishers who also are disappointed with the quality of fishery management, the quality of the water in North Carolina, and the quality of political representation.

The irony of the Chowan fishers and other fishers in the state is that their love of home, and the very feelings of attachment to the estuary that encourage stewardship and resource conservation, are the qualities of their livelihoods that prevent the emergence of effective coalitions of fishers. Too often their knowledge of fish, shellfish, substrates, and water quality is too rooted in a local ecosystem to marshal an effective challenge to conventional authority based on the more general principles of biology or fishery science. The detailed, rooted nature of the environmental knowledge of fishers allows fishery biologists and economists in the state to discount that knowledge, in whole or in part, as not based on the tried-and-true methods of science: repeated observation, experimentation, controlled settings, and so forth.

My friend, neighbor, and colleague Don Stanley, a biologist with a sophisticated understanding of ecology, observes that people often talk as though they are separate from, rather than a part of, the environment.

Unfortunately, much of fishery science, in particular the fisheries biology and economics that are used to draft government fishery policies, encourages scientists to run their tests and draw their conclusions as though fishers and fish moved in two separate environments, or as though fishers' incomes were separate from fishers' lives as husbands, fathers, and sons, or as though fishers themselves somehow existed outside the ebbs and flows of local history.

Here lies a second irony: science often treats things as though they are separate in experiments or experimental settings, yet bases those experiments on general principles, theories, that supposedly join together, explain, and predict all kinds of behaviors. By contrast, fishers view the environment holistically, as a whole made up of interrelated parts that often behave chaotically, but find it difficult to articulate the behaviors of fish or the quality of the water in terms of more abstract theoretical principles of science. Consider the following observations by Parker Creeley, a crabber from Pamlico County, talking about the death of hundreds of crabs one summer:

Well, the crabs died in there with us. The first time in fifteen years that I've ever had crabs die on me down there. And they died right on up. Normally up this river here, if you're getting less than 3 feet of water, you don't have no problems with the crabs dying in the pots when you have one of these kills come through. Down there with us, it didn't matter how deep you were or how shallow you were. The crabs were still dying.

Before they done that, about three days before that, I'd seen a crop duster spraying up in the open farm fields up in there. You could see him a-spraying over the treetops and mess there. And then we had a large rain come through. . . . About a couple of days after that, the crabs went to dying up in the head of the bays and it just worked right out of the bays. Everyday you'd see it coming down the bay a little bit further and a little bit further. And it took about two and a half weeks to go through there. And when it got down where the crabs didn't die, there just weren't no crabs. What it didn't kill, it run out of there.

Parker's observations, suggesting a relationship between crop dusting and the death of crabs, were made over a period of several days through one summer and based on previous observations of crab behaviors in different depths of water and different locations in the estuary. They were, then, repeated observations, yet observations conducted not in experimental or laboratory settings but in the natural context in which they take place. In the estuary, you cannot hold constant salinity levels, nutrient mixtures, rates of water flow, or other factors that might affect the crabs. When Parker talks about his observations, he does so in everyday terms, making common grammatical errors, repeating himself, at times seeming to slip around inside his sentences, watering down any authority of voice that he might have achieved with statistical evidence and the terse sentences of science.

It is that kind of scientific authority—and the credentialism and educational ethnocentrism that justify this authority—that allowed the Division of Marine Fisheries to discount what the Chowan fishers had to say. Yet scientific authority is often achieved at the expense of serious, critical, creative thought. Too often, scientific authority is assumed to be superior to any other authority because it packages ideas in standard methods of gaining and passing along knowledge. So standardized, the methods of science become easy to pass around, easy to use as the standard currency of authority.

If we think of science as authority's standard currency, we need only take a second metaphorical step to consider the influence it wields over all other voices. Paul Bohannan, a fine anthropologist, learned from the Tiv of Nigeria that the British disrupted the Tiv economy by introducing the idea and instruments of a single currency, replacing three theaters of trade with a single measure, a single standard. Before the British, Tiv traded agricultural produce and the daily fare of living in one theater of exchange; their coveted cattle, decorated textiles, and brass rods in a second theater of exchange; and people—wives and children but not slaves—in a third. It was as unthinkable for Tiv to trade cattle for yams, or brass rods for daughters, as it is for us to trade a son for a Mercedes, or a revered grandmother's cameo for a ticket to the Super Bowl. When the British introduced money to the Tiv, the Tiv tried to confine its use to the sphere of trade in provisions, resisting the idea and practice of valuing cattle, textiles, brass, women, and children by the single measure of the English pound. The Tiv were so morally outraged at British attempts to use pounds to purchase their beloved cattle that they came to despise pounds, dollars, francs, marks, and other currencies altogether. Tiv resistance stirred the British to cruelty as they undertook the slow, painful creation of the Nigerian state, a process that involved suppression of other voices along with alternative theaters of trade.

The failure of the Division of Marine Fisheries to take the Chowan fishers seriously, cutting them out of the policy-making process, was another way of suppressing an alternative voice, an alternative authority. It was a subtle yet effective exercise of power. Based on highly regarded scientific principles, packaged in calm and measured voices, backed by college degrees and certificates and other credentials, the Division continued issuing proclamations about the herring fishery as though no one, least of all those dependent on the fishery, had ever objected to its ruling. They behaved as if Gabe and his neighbors did not exist.

In recent years, a mountain of literature has been produced by anthropologists, sociologists, political scientists, and others on the question of resistance, resistance of slaves against the authority of their masters, serfs against lords, wives against abusive husbands—in short, the weak resisting the strong. Much of this literature can be traced to the often dense, turgid writings of internationally known scholars like Michel Foucault, or the somewhat easier-to-follow examples of less well known anthropologist James Scott, who wrote about "everyday" forms of resistance that he witnessed first among the peasants in Asia, such as foot-dragging, sabotage, petty theft from bosses, and pretending to misunderstand commands.

Those writing about resistance would probably concur that the Chowan fishers will continue to struggle against the authorities. Yet for struggles like those of Gabe Bishop and the Chowan fishers, more inspirational than the writings of men like Foucault and Scott are the stories that surface again and again in a variety of forms, with a variety of characters, evoking the same feelings of triumph that most of us feel when we see someone overcoming exceptional hardship. I refer to the stories that are variations on the setting and times and characters of David and Goliath, that foretell the meek inheriting the earth, that praise the ant over the grasshopper. These are the stories of underdogs, of a simple son named Jack who climbs a beanstalk, of a king tithing jewels but a pauper's meager shillings opening the gates of heaven, of an old man alone at sea landing a fish the length of his vessel. These are the stories that stir Gabe and his neighbors to action. These are the tales that keep alive the sense that no one is powerless, that no matter how large, how well-financed, how well-connected your opponents, there is a chance that cleverness and perseverance will prevail. Among fishers like Gabe, it is the sense that your dearest possession, your heritage, will give you the authority of voice to win others to your cause.

Yet the irony of Gabe and his neighbors, of most commercial fishers of North Carolina and in other parts of the world, is that their very strength is also a source of weakness. As deeply as their roots reach into the estuary's gifts, their failure may lie in the everyday nature of their resistance, the everyday justice they insist on, the polite words and phrases of generosity, and the giving and receiving of gifts. The irony of the honest and moral nature of this struggle is that they risk becoming too mired in local history and local circumstances to marshal an effective or lasting challenge to established voices of established authority. They risk sending roots too far inward to branch outward, to link arms and causes with other commercial fishers and others who are concerned, deeply concerned, about the estuary's gifts.

Yet for all their weaknesses, commercial fishers today are our best hope for a diversified, interesting, clean Mid-Atlantic Coast. They are the estuary's gift to us, and it is they who—collectively, joined with others concerned about the estuary—may be the David who succeeds in slaying the Goliaths of phosphate miners, forestry and corporate hog executives, and the real-estate developers who deface our coast with condominiums. It is they who may best serve those who fight against the forces that daily, everyday, bit by bit by bit, divest us of our coast, our heritage, our very opportunity to repay the estuary's gifts.

BIBLIOGRAPHIC ESSAY

Inevitably, the history and contemporary setting of any place that people have inhabited for thousands of years will be rich and deeply interesting. Local stories, family histories, daily struggles and celebrations, and feats of survival are every bit as fascinating as the grand histories of, say, the Civil War or the conferences of major political leaders. Appreciating the history and daily life of such places, especially when exploding bombs or military bands are not demanding the attention of thousands, requires a sense of the lived experiences of individuals and families much the same way one needs to acquire a taste for fine literature because of its richness and complexity. Much of the anthropology, and a good deal of recent work by historians, has been devoted to writing local history and locating the daily struggles of working people within larger social and economic processes. I take these works as my lead.

CHAPTER I: ESTUARIES AND GIFTS

In North Carolina, one particularly notable historian in this regard has been David Cecelski, who has written extensively on the experiences of African-Americans in that state and whose essay "On the Shores of Freedom" (1994a; see also his work on Hyde County, *Along Freedom Road,* 1994b), along with William Still's collection about fugitive slaves' escapes, *The Underground Railroad* (1872), and Mark Taylor's historical work on North Carolina fisheries, "Seiners and Tongers" (1992), served as principal sources for the opening vignette of this book. Passages from Bland Simpson's *The Great Dismal* (1990) inspired many of the images and facts about Carolina and Virginia swamps, here and throughout the volume.

The central theme of this book, and its title, owe their origins primarily to Marcel Mauss's (1967 [1925]) classic work on the gift. Mauss's ideas have enjoyed increasing attention in recent years with an edited volume compiled by Arjun Appadurai (1986) and with Annette Weiner's (1992) work on "inalienable wealth" (that is, items that are valuable because they invoke either personal or cultural histories, such as a grandmother's bracelet or Yellowstone Park). Weiner's work has clarified "the paradox of keeping-while-giving" of gift exchange, and Antonius Robben's *Sons of the Sea Goddess*, about Brazilian canoe and boat fishers, gave me confidence that I could apply these ideas to household fishers of the Mid-Atlantic Coast.

For the biology and ecological information regarding the Albemarle-Pamlico Estuarine System (APES), more important than published sources have been my colleagues at East Carolina University's Institute for Coastal and Marine Resources, as well as many individuals who were at one time affiliated with the University of North Carolina Sea Grant College Program. Particularly helpful at the Institute for Coastal and Marine Resources have been Don Stanley, Bill Queen, Joe Luzscovich, Roger Rulifson, and Margie Gallagher. Current and former Sea Grant folk include B.J. Copeland, Kathy Hart, Ron Hodson, Jim Murray, Lundie Spence, Walter Clark, and Jim Bahen. A group of studies from the APES Studies, particularly the multiauthor description of the system, which actually consists of a series of short, easy-to-read descriptions of different parts of the system, provided the basic facts of the system's life.

CHAPTER 2: NAMES OF WATER

Much of the information for this chapter, as well as for Chapter 3, came from visits to the museums in Beaufort, Plymouth, and Elizabeth City and to the Division of Archives and History in Raleigh and the David Phelps Archeology Lab on the campus of East Carolina University. This chapter also draws heavily on several classic anthropological works, beginning with George Fraser's *The Golden Bough* and moving quickly to more recent works. The section on maps was inspired by the map collection of North Carolina's Division of Archives and History, which traces maps of the state through time, as well as Joel Makower's edited volume *The Map Catalog: Every Kind of Map and Chart on Earth and Even Some Above It* (1986). Benjamin Orlove's "Mapping Reeds and Reading Maps" (1991), an article about the significance of maps in disputes over territories of Lake Titicaca in the Andes, helped confirm several of my own suspicions about the importance of visual representations of landscapes to people who are involved in territorial disputes.

Several ethnohistorical and archaeological accounts contributed to this chapter as well. John Swanton's (1946) classic and monumental *Indians of the Southeastern United States,* along with short pieces by John Collier (1947) and Maurice Mook (1944), were quite helpful. David Phelps's (1993) overview of coastal Native American populations, along with others reprinted in the informative collection edited by Mark Mathis and Jeffrey Crow (1993), served as the primary source for chronology for this material, as did discussions with Dr. Phelps,

Charles Ewen, physical anthropologist Dale Hutchinson, and several students, particularly Charles Heath and Kimberly Zawacki.

The information on scapulamancy comes from a 1957 article by Omar Moore, "Divination: A New Perspective," yet more recent studies, such as Michael Chibnik's "Evolution of Cultural Rules" (1989), have demonstrated the importance of experimentation and repeated observations among preliterate peoples. Several more-recent works have focused on folk biology or ethnobiology, much of which comes from cultural ecology (for example, Johnson and Griffith 1995). The book of readings on folk management by James McGoodwin and Christopher Dyer (1994) was also helpful here.

In both this chapter and the following, Charles Heath's excellent master's thesis (1997), which I had the privilege to direct, synthesized much of the previous work on herring fishing and added important new oral historical accounts. Eric Wolf's (1982) work on the North American fur trade served as a cornerstone of this chapter, and his work inspires mine along with the work of an entire generation of anthropologists. Indeed, it is difficult to count among colleagues my own age more than a handful who have not read and reread his *Europe and the People Without History*, which is without a doubt the most influential book in anthropology of the last quarter of the twentieth century. Anthropologists who have not had the pleasure of reading this work have little hope of making any significant contributions to anthropological thought.

CHAPTER 3: EARLY FISHERIES, OILY FISHERIES

This chapter draws heavily on several local and regional publications about North Carolina's fisheries and fishing communities, many of them published privately, in limited editions, or in somewhat obscure places. Not available in bookstores for the general reader, they can be found in such outlets as coastal museums, gift shops, and cultural resource centers in Raleigh. Exceptions to this are several works published by the University of North Carolina Press, including Bland Simpson's *The Great Dismal: A Carolinian's Swamp Memoir* (1990), Alton Ballance's *Ocracokers* (1989), and David Stick's *Outer Banks of North Carolina* (1958).

Equally helpful were several books and pamphlets by North Carolina's Division of Archives and History, whose list of publications has flourished under Jeffrey Crow's excellent taste and writing skill. "Whaling on the North Carolina Coast," by Marcus and Sallie Simpson (1990), was extremely useful for this chapter, as was Mark Taylor's 1992 article entitled "Seiners and Tongers: North Carolina Fisheries in the Old and New South." Taylor also led me to Boyce's book on Chowan County (1917) and Porter Crayon's delightful 1857 article in *Harper's*.

Less widely distributed are Kay Holt Roberts Stephens's two-volume set on Salter Path, *Judgment Land* (1984, 1989), Pat Garber's *Ocracoke Wild: A Naturalist's Year on an Outer Banks Island* (1995), and Carl Goerch's *Ocracoke* (1995). These books were helpful not only for this chapter, but also for later chapters on the fisheries of North Carolina.

CHAPTER 4: VANISHING WOMEN

This chapter is based primarily on my own work on labor in low-wage industries, including work on seafood-processing houses in North Carolina, Maryland, and Virginia, as well as studies of other food-processing industries in the midwestern United States and in the American South. Three books emerged from these studies and the studies of others working on similar issues of immigration, community, and low-wage work. The first, *Jones's Minimal Low-Wage Labor in the United States* (Griffith 1993), compares seafood and poultry workers in the southeastern United States. The second, *Working Poor: Farmworkers in the United States* (Griffith et al. 1995), discusses the growing importance of labor contracting, labor control, and other attributes of farm labor in seven regions of the United States. The third, *Any Way They Cut It: Food Processing and Small Town America* (Stull, Broadway, and Griffith, 1995), is an edited volume of case studies about how food-processing companies, primarily meat- and poultry-processing firms, have changed several small towns and rural counties across the country. Sahlins's *Stone Age Economics* (1972), still a classic among anthropologists, influenced my ideas about the different ways labor power can be utilized and the various perceptions people have of alternative uses of human labor.

For its overall sensitivity to the business of crabbing and crab picking, William Warner's *Beautiful Swimmers: Watermen, Crabs, and the Chesapeake Bay* has no equal.

The case of the Mexican women who were mistreated by the owners of seafood-processing houses in Maryland and North Carolina came from the legal paperwork (depositions, trial transcripts, and so on) that were associated with the trial that Labor Secretary Martin brought against seafood processors in North Carolina and Maryland.

The sections on worker resistance come primarily from James Scott's work, *Weapons of the Weak: Everyday Forms of Peasant Resistance* (1978), but work on resistance among the downtrodden has become such a prevailing theme in anthropology that it is difficult to tease out much of the work that informed this discussion. I have found the recent work of Mark Moberg and Christopher

Dyer (1995) helpful, as well as Aiwa Ong's (1987) study of factory women in Malaysia.

CHAPTERS 5 AND 6: FISHING IN THE BALANCE, AND THE FISHERIES

I discuss these two chapters together because the sources that informed these chapters overlap so much it would be repetitive to discuss them separately. Work on conflicts between recreational and commercial fishers, as well as on how recreational fishers perceive commercial fishers, came primarily from several studies I conducted either by myself or with others, principally my buddy Jeff Johnson: Johnson and Griffith 1985, 1995; Griffith 1996; and Griffith and Maiolo 1989. Information on North Carolina fisheries came primarily from three studies conducted for the North Carolina Moratorium Steering Committee: Garrity-Blake 1996; Griffith 1996; and Johnson and Orbach 1996. My own study (1996) was very helpful too because its information was so familiar to me. The Johnson and Orbach report provided statistics on the fisheries but failed to facilitate the formulation of objective policy recommendations. Barbara Garrity-Blake's work on the menhaden fishery (1994), the finest work published to date on a North Carolina fishery, inspired much in these chapters.

Several other works published recently about fishing have influenced this work. These include Durrenberger (1993, 1996), LiPuma and Meltzoff (1997), Maril (1995), Sider (1987), Vickers (1994), Acheson and McCay (1987), Acheson (1992), and Griffith and Dyer (1994). These works, among others, have surpassed much earlier work based primarily on outdated microeconomic assumptions and modernization theory, including Hardin's "tragedy of the commons" thesis. Until Acheson's work on Maine, most of the work on fisheries in the United States was of extremely poor quality, although several works about peasant fisheries and Canadian fisheries made important discoveries. Since Acheson, much of the work on fisheries has benefited from an influx of anthropologists who have had experience studying fishers and farmers in other cultural settings, particularly Bonnie McCay and Paul Durrenberger. It is unfortunate that the legacy of the earlier work remains only in the form of editorial positions or influence in academic journals dealing with coastal peoples. For this reason, the best anthropological work on coastal peoples is usually not found in the pages of *Coastal Zone Management* or similar journals but in the journals *American Ethnologist* and in *Human Organization.*

CHAPTER 7: REWRITING THE COAST

The materials for this chapter were assembled primarily with the help of Walter Clark, an attorney for the University of North Carolina's Sea Grant College

Program, who prepared a detailed manuscript for me about coastal property issues. It was he who pointed me to the 1892 Supreme Court decision and clarified aspects of the authority of the Coastal Zone Management Act. The information on the West Palm Beach neighborhood called Northwood comes from my own research, which was sponsored by the National Science Foundation and published in Griffith (1995). Two biographies of Henry Flagler (Akin 1988 and Chandler 1986) helped in understanding the man himself, but both conveniently left out Flagler's role in the burning of the Styx. That was included in a locally produced book, *Like a Mighty Banyan,* and in a series of articles about African-Americans in Palm Beach in the *Palm Beach Post.*

The issue of the *Kenyon Review* edited by Lewis Hyde was released in 1997 (vol. 19, no. 1, Winter) and includes several articles that informed the idea of history as territory. The quotation from Hyde is from pages i–ii.

CHAPTER 8: VERSIONS OF HOME

With the exception of Paul Bohannan's fine work on the Tiv (1968), most of this chapter was based on original research and personal experiences. The experiences in south central Florida came from work I did in the late 1980s and early 1990s while preparing materials for *Working Poor* (Griffith et al. 1995).

REFERENCES

Acheson, James. 1992. *The Lobster Gangs of Maine*. Boston: University Press of New England.

Acheson, James, and Bonnie McCay. 1987. *The Question of the Commons*. Tucson: University of Arizona Press.

Akin, Edward. 1988. *Flagler: Rockefeller Partner and Robber Baron*. Gainesville: University of Florida Press.

Appadurai, Arjun. 1986. *The Social Life of Things*. Cambridge: Cambridge University Press.

Ballance, Alton. 1989. *Ocracokers*. Chapel Hill: University of North Carolina Press.

Bell, Marvin. 1977. *Stars Which See, Stars Which Do Not See*. New York: Atheneum.

Bellow, Saul. 1978. *Humboldt's Gift*. New York: Penguin.

Bohannan, Paul. 1968. "Some Principles of Exchange and Investment Among the Tiv." In E. LeClair and H. Schneider, eds., *Economic Anthropology*, 300310. New York: Holt, Rinehart & Winston.

Bourdier, Pierre. 1977. *Outline of a Theory of Practice*. Cambridge: Cambridge University Press.

Boyce, W. Scott. 1917. *Economic and Social History of Chowan County, North Carolina, 1880–1915*. New York: Columbia University Press.

Byrd, John. 1991. *Taphonomy, Diversity, and Seasonality of Cashie Phase Faunal Assemblages from the Jordan's Landing Site, 31BR7, North Carolina*. Master's thesis, Department of Anthropology, University of Tennessee, Knoxville, Tenn.

Cecelski, David. 1994a. "The Shores of Freedom: The Maritime Underground Railroad in North Carolina, 1800–1861." *North Carolina Historical Review* 71 (2): 174–206.

———. 1994b. *Along Freedom Road: Hyde County, North Carolina, and the Fate of Black Schools in the South*. Chapel Hill: University of North Carolina Press.

Chandler, David Leon. 1986. *Henry Flagler: The Astonishing Life and Times of the Visionary Robber Baron Who Founded Florida.* New York: Macmillan Company.

Chibnik, Michael. 1989. "The Evolution of Cultural Rules." *Journal of Anthropological Research* 17 (4): 320–33.

Collier, John. 1947. *Indians of the Americas.* New York: New American Library and Mentor Books.

Crayon, Porter. 1857. "North Carolina Illustrated: The Fisheries." *Harper's New Monthly Magazine* 7 (March): 57–72

Daniel, Randy I. 1998. *Hardaway Revisited.* Tuscaloosa: University of Alabama Press.

Durrenberger, E. Paul. 1993. *It's All Politics: South Alabama's Seafood Industry.* Urbana: University of Illinois Press.

———. 1996. *Gulf Coast Soundings: People and Policy in the Mississippi Shrimp Industry.* Lawrence: University Press of Kansas.

Foucault, Michel. 1971. *The History of Sexuality.* Vol. 1. New York: Penguin.

Garber, Pat. 1995. *Ocracoke Wild: A Naturalist's Year on an Outer Banks Island.* Asheboro, N.C.: Down Home Press.

Garcia Marquez, Gabriel. 1971. *One Hundred Years of Solitude.* New York: Avon Books.

Gardner, Paul. 1990. *Excavations at the Amity Site.* Final Report of the Pomeiooc Project. East Carolina University Archaeological Report 7, Greenville, N.C.

Garrity-Blake, Barbara. 1994. *The Fish Factory: Work and Meaning Among Black and White Fishermen of the American Menhaden Industry.* Knoxville: University of Tennessee Press.

———. 1996. "Occupational Transition Among the Fishermen of Carteret County, North Carolina." Report to the North Carolina Moratorium Steering Committee, Raleigh, University of North Carolina Sea Grant College Program.

Goerch, Carl. 1995. *Ocracoke.* Winston-Salem, N.C.: John Blair.

Griffith, David. 1993. *Jones's Minimal: Low-Wage Labor in the United States.* Albany: State University of New York Press.

———. 1995. "Names of Death." *American Anthropologist* 97 (3): 453–56.

———. 1996. *Fishers of North Carolina: A Classificatory Analysis.* Report to the North Carolina Moratorium Steering Committee, Raleigh, University of North Carolina Sea Grant College Program.

Griffith, David, and Christopher Dyer. 1994. "Social and Economic Impact of New Regulations in the Northeast Groundfish Fishing Industry." NOAH, Final Report. Wood's Hole, Massachusetts.

REFERENCES

Griffith, David, Ed Kissam, Jeronimo Camposeco, Anna Garcia, David Runsten, and Manuel Valdes Pizzini. 1995. *Working Poor: Farmworkers in the United States.* Philadelphia: Temple University Press.

Griffith, David, and John Maiolo. 1989. "Conflicts Among Trap Fishers in the South Atlantic." *City and Society* 3 (1): 74–88.

Hardin, Garrett. 1968. "The Tragedy of the Commons." *Science* 162: 124348.

Heath, Charles. 1997. "A Cultural History of River Herring and Shad Fisheries in Eastern North Carolina: The Prehistoric Period Through the Twentieth Century." Master's thesis, Department of Anthropology, East Carolina University, Greenville, North Carolina.

Hyde, Lewis. 1997. "American Memory, American Forgetfulness. . . ." *Kenyon Review* 19 (1): i–iii.

Johnson, Jeffrey, and David Griffith. 1985. *Perceptions of Marine Fish: A Study of Recreational Fishermen in the U.S. Southeast.* University of North Carolina Sea Grant College Program Technical Report 85–101, Raleigh.

———. 1995. "Seafood, Pollution, and the Distribution of Cultural Knowledge." *Human Ecology* 24 (1): 87–108.

Johnson, Jeffrey, and Michael Orbach. 1996. *North Carolina Fisheries.* Technical Report Prepared for the North Carolina Moratorium Steering Committee: Data and Analytical Section. Greenville and Raleigh: ICMR and UNC Sea Grant Technical Report.

Keillor, Garrison. 1982. *Happy to Be Here.* New York: Atheneum.

Kelly, Richard, and Barbara Kelly. 1993. *The Carolina Watermen: Bug Hunters and Boat Builders.* Winston-Salem, N.C.: John F. Blair.

LiPuma, Edward, and Sarah Meltzoff. 1997. "The Cross-Currents of Ethnicity and Class in the Construction of Public Policy." *American Ethnologist* 24 (1): 114–31.

Makower, Joel. 1986. *The Map Catalog: Every Kind of Map and Chart on Earth and Even Some Above It.* New York: Vintage Books.

Mathis, Mark, and Jeffrey Crow, eds. 1993 (1983). *The Prehistory of North Carolina: An Archaeological Symposium.* Raleigh, N.C.: Division of Archives and History.

Mauss, Marcel. 1967 (1925). *The Gift: Forms and Functions of Exchange in Archaic Societies.* New York: W. W. Norton & Company.

McGoodwin, James, and Christopher Dyer. 1994. *Folk Management in the World's Fisheries.* Boulder: University Press of Colorado.

Michener, James. 1978. *Chesapeake.* New York: Random House.

Moberg, Mark, and Christopher Dyer. 1995. "The Moral Economy of Resistance." *Human Organization* 54 (1): 83–88.

Mook, Maurice. 1944. "Algonkin Ethnohistory of the Carolina Sound." *Journal of the Washington Academy of Sciences* 34:6–7.

Moore, Omar K. 1957. "Divination: A New Perspective." *American Anthropologist* 59 (1): 69–74.

Newman, Katherine. 1988. *Falling from Grace: The Experience of Downward Mobility in the American Middle Class.* New York: The Free Press.

Ong, Aiwa. 1987. *Spirits of Resistance and Capitalist Discipline: Factory Workers in Malaysia.* Albany: State University of New York Press.

Orlove, Benjamin. 1991. "Mapping Reeds and Reading Maps: The Politics of Representation in Lake Titicaca." *American Ethnologist* 18 (1): 3–38.

Phelps, David. 1993 (1983). "Archaeology of the North Carolina Coast and Coastal Plain: Problems and Hypotheses." In M. Mathis and J. Crow, eds., *The Prehistory of North Carolina: An Archaeological Symposium,* 153. Raleigh, N.C.: Division of Archives and History.

Rawlings, Marjorie Kinnans. 1942. *Cross Creek.* New York: Charles Scribner's Sons.

Redford, Dorothy. 1988. *Sommerset Homecoming: Renewing a Lost Heritage.* New York: Doubleday.

Robbens, Antonius. 1989. *Sons of the Sea Goddess.* New York: Columbia University Press.

Roundtree, Helen. 1975. "Change Came Slowly: The Case of the Powatan Indians of Virginia. " *Journal of Ethnic Studies* 3 (3): 119.

Sahlins, Marshal. 1972. *Stone Age Economics.* Chicago: Aldine Publishers.

Scott, James. 1978. *Weapons of the Weak: Everyday Forms of Peasant Resistance.* New Haven: Yale University Press.

Sider, Gerald. 1987. *Culture and Class in Anthropology and History: A Newfoundland Illustration.* Cambridge: Cambridge University Press.

Simpson, Bland. 1990. *The Great Dismal: A Carolinian's Swamp Memoir.* Chapel Hill: University of North Carolina Press.

Simpson, Marcus, and Sallie Simpson. 1990. *Whaling on North Carolina's Coast.* Raleigh, N.C.: Division of Archives and History.

Stephens, Kay Holt Roberts. 1984. *Judgment Land.* vol. 1. Havelock, N.C.: The Print Shop.

Stepick, Alex, and Guiermo Grenier. 1992. *Miami, Now! Immigration, Ethnicity, and Social Change.* Gainesville: University of Florida Press.

Stepick, Alex, and Alejandro Portes. 1993. *City on the Edge: The Transformation of Miami.* Berkeley and Los Angeles: University of California Press.

Steward, Julian. 1938. *Basin-Plateau Aboriginal Sociopolitical Groups.* Bureau of American Ethnology Bulletin 120. Washington, D.C.: U.S. Government Printing Office.

Stick, David. 1952. *Graveyard of the Atlantic.* Chapel Hill: University of North Carolina Press.

———. 1958. *The Outer Banks of North Carolina.* Chapel Hill: University of North Carolina Press.

Still, William. 1872. *The Underground Rail Road: A Record of Facts, Authentic Narratives, Letters, &c., Narrating the Hardships, Hair-Breadth Escapes, and Death Struggles of the Slaves in Their Efforts for Freedom.* Philadelphia: Porter & Coates.

Stull, Donald, Michael Broadway, and David Griffith. 1995. *Any Way They Cut It: Food Processing and Small Town America.* Lawrence: University Press of Kansas.

Swanton, John. 1946. *Indians of the Southeastern United States.* Bureau of American Ethnology Bulletin 137. Washington, D.C.: U.S. Government Printing Office.

Taylor, Mark. 1992. "Seiners and Tongers: North Carolina Fisheries in the Old and New South." *North Carolina Historical Review* 69 (1): 1–36.

Warner, William. 1976. *Beautiful Swimmers: Watermen, Crabs, and the Chesapeake Bay* New York: Atlantic Monthly Press Books (Little, Brown & Company).

Weiner, Annette. 1992. *Inalienable Wealth.* Berkeley and Los Angeles: University of California Press.

Whedbee, Charles Harry. 1966. *Legends of the Outer Banks and Tar Heel Tidewater.* Winston-Salem, N.C.: John F. Blair.

Whitehead, Donald. 1972. "Developmental and Environmental History of the Dismal Swamp." *Ecological Monographs* 42:301–15.

Wolf, Eric. 1982. *Europe and the People Without History.* Berkeley and Los Angeles: University of California Press.

INDEX

INDEX